The Half-Breed Rival, The Tangled Trail: A Tale Of The Settlements

Joseph E. Badger Jr.

In the interest of creating a more extensive selection of rare historical book reprints, we have chosen to reproduce this title even though it may possibly have occasional imperfections such as missing and blurred pages, missing text, poor pictures, markings, dark backgrounds and other reproduction issues beyond our control. Because this work is culturally important, we have made it available as a part of our commitment to protecting, preserving and promoting the world's literature. Thank you for your understanding.

Copyrighted, 1887, by BEADLE AND ADAMS. Entered at the Post Office at New York, N. Y., as Second Class Mail Matter. Jan. 29, 1887.

Vol. XII. $2.50 a Year. Published Weekly by Beadle and Adams, No. 98 WILLIAM ST., NEW YORK. Price, Five Cents. No. 146.

"GENTLEMEN, I MUST BEG YOUR INDULGENCE FOR INTERRUPTING YOUR COUNCIL SO ABRUPTLY."

The Half-Breed Rival;
OR,
THE TANGLED TRAIL.

A Tale of the Settlements.

BY JOS. E. BADGER, JR.,

AUTHOR OF "MARIPOSA MARSH," "THE PRAIRIE RANCH," "THE COLORADO BOYS," "THE TIGER HUNTERS," ETC., ETC.

CHAPTER I.
THE HIDDEN VOICE.

"WELL, gentlemen, I propose we get to business. I for one have no time to waste, and there are plenty of us present for a beginning," and the speaker glanced approvingly around the room.

He was a tall, powerfully-built man, aged probably forty-five years, of a rugged, yet intelligent and almost handsome cast of features; while the rough "home-made" garments that he wore disguised without hiding the splendid contour of his form. There was the slightest possible tinge of the "brogue" to his speech, that would have told a close observer the land of his nativity.

"I second the motion," piped out a shrill, quavering voice, as a tall, skeleton-like body abruptly shot up to its full hight, and then sunk down with a jar upon his stool, as all eyes were turned upon the speaker, while he vehemently scrubbed at his face with an enormous yellow cotton handkerchief, to hide the confusion he felt at thus "speaking out in meeting."

"Thank you, friend Hannibal Hooker," bowed the first speaker. "But first we will have something to— Landlord! Jim Henderson, I say!" roared out he who appeared to take the lead in the meeting, bringing down his huge, sun-browned, toil-hardened fist upon the table before him, with such force, that it seemed as if the deal would split, while Hannibal Hooker leaped convulsively from his stool with a faint squeak.

"Thunder 'n' lightnin', Cap'n Neil," uttered a deep, rumbling voice, as the door opened and a man thrust his head through the aperture, "am I deaf. thet you need to t'ar the house down? What d'ye want?" and he entered the room.

It was like a mouse with a lion's voice. Scarcely five feet, and built in proportion, the new-comer spoke with a voice such as we imagine the giant Magog to have used, it was so full, deep and sonorous. But, if not consistent with his body, it was with his heart, for "Honest Jim Henderson" was a by-word, for use to typify truth and fidelity, among his neighbors.

"Bring us something hot and hearty, avic, for our throats will need wetting before we get through," responded he whom the landlord called Captain Neil.

"I protest, gentlemen! I protest most emphatically against this proceeding!" exclaimed a short, rotund personage, bouncing upon his chair the better to be observed. "Must we depend upon intoxicating liquors to enable us to form our plans? I say no, a thousand times no! With such supports, our downfall—"

What the conclusion of this worthy personage's speech was, is lost to posterity, for by some mischance—it *was* said, by the adroit trip of a neighbor's *foot*—the stool upon which he stood was overturned, and the little fat fellow plunged headlong beneath the table, giving utterance to a series of grunts and snorts that in no wise tended to quell the shouts of merriment at his mishap.

"There, Brother Bacon," laughed the leader, "is a flat contradiction to your argument. You fall by opposing it; we will stand with its aid."

The worthy brother made no further objection, and when the punch was brought in, by mere legerdemain, a cup filled with the steaming beverage found itself tightly clasped in his chubby hand, and ten minutes later was empty. Then Captain Neil stood up and spoke:

"My friends and neighbors: Most of you know what is our purpose in gathering here to-night, but as a few may not, I will briefly state the facts. You all know that for nearly a year past we have been troubled with floods of counterfeit money, and with losing our stock. How this is done so secretly, and who by, is yet for us to learn. But one thing is certain: unless we *do* find out, and that soon, we may as well sell out for what we can get, and leave the country.

"Not one, so far as I can tell, among us all, but have suffered in both ways; for my part, I am five thousand dollars poorer to-night than I was five months since. Now, must this state of affairs continue? I, for one, say *no!*—a thousand times no: and if need be, will spend every moment of my time for the purpose of ferreting out these scoundrels.

"But to come to the point; what I have to propose is this: We must organize a band—a *Vigilance Committee.* Do you know what that means? They had one in Kentucky—they had one in Arkansas; we must have one in Kansas! Judge Lynch has jurisdiction *here* as well as elsewhere, and it is to him we must turn, since the law of the land is powerless to protect us!

"All who are now present we can trust, I believe, and there are others who can be admitted. But you must act cautiously, and know every man well before he becomes a member. One traitor among us would counteract all the good that others might do. But all this you know as well as I; and those who wish to speak, or who have any plan to propose, will now be heard," concluded Neil McGuire, as he resumed his seat, and filled the well-blackened corn-cob pipe that lay before him.

Several of the members delivered their opinions upon the subject, all agreeing with their leader that something must be done; the only thing in doubt, appeared to be in deciding what that thing should be. It was while the debate was at its hight, that loud, excited voices were heard in the bar-room without, followed by the sounds of a scuffle, with a rattle of overturned chairs and tables.

Then the connecting door was violently thrust open, without the trouble being taken of lifting the latch, and a man stood upon the threshold, keenly scrutinizing the scene before him. A man, we said, but it might well have been, a remarkable man.

So tall that the hair of his uncovered head touched the top of the doorway, and yet so perfectly proportioned that had it not been for the standard to compare by, he would not have seemed over six feet, if so much. The hands that grasped the sides of the doorway were large and muscular, but as fine and white as a lady's; and from the position, great masses of swelling muscle could be seen distending the light material of his sack coat, upon the arms.

His face was of a massive style of beauty, and yet not without delicate lines and touches. The keen blue eyes were large and frank-looking, usually having a genial, good-humored tone about them that instinctively attracted the beholder; but which had now given place to a cold, steel-like glitter that warned how dangerous it might be to cross his mood.

In age he appeared about thirty, and but for the long, flowing mustache and beard of a soft flaxen color, one would have taken him for half a decade less. After a few moments' silence the intruder spoke, in a full, clear tone that would have been musical had it not been for the metallic ring, occasioned by his anger or excitement.

"Gentlemen, I must beg your indulgence for interrupting your council so abruptly, but 'Honest Jim' Blockhead yonder denied me admittance, and as I was in no mood for arguing the case, I fear I gave the fellow a broken head, and took the liberty of introducing myself."

"You say right," responded Neil McGuire, in a stern tone, as he confronted the stranger, "it *is* a liberty. We were engaged upon private business, that does not concern you in the least, and—"

"Pardon, my dear sir," interrupted the stranger, "and allow me to correct you. The business you were upon *does* concern me, and I doubt if one man present is more deeply interested in its success than myself," he added, in a conciliatory tone, that was flatly contradicted by the glitter of his eyes at the manner of McGuire.

"Perhaps you will tell me where you got your knowledge of what we were consulting upon, and your reasons for this intrusion," coldly returned the latter.

"It is easily done," quoth the stranger, as he advanced to the table and coolly filling a pint cup with the punch, drained it at a draught, not heeding the scowls of those around him, "and shall be as you say. In the first place, you are organizing a league to put down the horsethieves and counterfeiters that infest us."

"Go on," was the cold reply.

"You are prudent, and I don't blame you. Who knows but what I am a spy, a person in the interest of those same scoundrels?" laughed the intruder.

"Just so; who *does* know?" chimed in a voice from among the crowd.

The man sprung to his feet and glared in the direction of the voice, but every face wore an expression of astonishment, while each man glanced around him as if to discover the speaker.

"If the fellow who spoke thus will be honest enough to show his face, perhaps he will —— who and what Clay Poynter is. I would —"

"How much — in *counterfeit money?*" squeaked a shrill treble from another part of the room, toward which Poynter turned in a frenzy of rage and fury.

"Peace, gentlemen!" ordered McGuire, thumping upon the table to give emphasis to his words. "We are not here for squabbling, but upon serious business. Mr. Poynter is a gentleman. Let him proceed."

"Gentlemen, it is true I am a comparative stranger among you, but, for all that, you have no occasion to insult me. I will give a hundred dollars to the man that will point me out the scoundrel who spoke those words!"

"Which will only cost you sixteen dollars!" added another voice—alluding to the general price paid for counterfeit money since the days of Sturdevant—sounding from close behind him, who had called himself Clay Poynter.

The latter swiftly turned, hissing out a bitter oath, with right arm drawn back to deal a fearful blow upon his insulter, *but no person was there!* The space behind him had been unoccupied since his entrance. Poynter staggered back against the table with a half-startled, half-puzzled look upon his features; but this he soon banished, and with a somewhat constrained voice, said:

"Really, the devil seems to be at work here to-night, and has selected me for his mark!"

"Never fear; he will not claim you yet. The mortgage has several weeks yet to run," again added the strange voice.

"Come—come!" impatiently cried McGuire, "this is all nonsense. Please go on with your explanation, Mr. Poynter."

"Well, I learned that you were about to organize a Vigilance Committee, and thought I would present my name for a membership. So I rode over from my house, and as I passed the ford at the creek, I was knocked from the saddle, and when I recovered, I was robbed of my horse as well as watch and a large sum of money."

"Ho, ho! the robber robbed!" croaked the mysterious voice, and the cry appeared to float around the room above the company's heads, most of whom were deathly pale, while anxious, apprehensive glances ran from one to another. "Ho, ho! the robber robbed!"

"Our worthy friend is quite a ventriloquist," slowly uttered Poynter, as his fiery eyes roved around the room, dwelling slightly upon each face; but upon one in particular he cast a glance of mingled hatred and triumph, then passed to another. "I would willingly give half I am worth, just to take one lesson from him," dwelling with bitter emphasis upon each word.

"Well, friends, we may as well break off now before harm is done," said Neil McGuire, in a vexed tone. "There's something wrong here, and the less we say, perhaps the better it will be, for who can have any object in breaking up this meeting, unless he or they are connected with this accused gang of scoundrels?"

"But what! must we give up the plan after all this to do?" exclaimed Demetrius Bacon, again leaping upon his stool in order to gain the desired auditory, forgetful of his late downfall.

"Give up the devil!" retorted McGuire, who

was not always precise in his language. "When I put my hand to a thing in dead up-and-down earnest, it's bound to go through. And now listen, all of you. Until you hear from me, attend to your business as usual, and do not make what has happened to-night the subject of conversation. We must use a little more circumspection, for if a spy can enter among us here we will need all our wits."

"I show you the spy—why don't you take him?" again squeaked the strange voice, and then as each man glanced at his neighbor, it added: "His name, *now*, is Clay Poynter!"

"My dear sir, whoever you may chance to be," cried the man thus strangely denounced, in an assumed tone of *nonchalant* politeness, as he glanced around the room, "I made an error a few moments since. I said that I would give half I am worth; so I will add the other moiety, if you grant me an interview."

There was no reply to this speech, and the party filed through the doorway into the bar-room of the "Twin Sycamores," the majority of them pausing to take a parting drink before leaving for home. Beside Neil McGuire stood a medium-sized man, of a sandy complexion, and who appeared to belong to a different class from the rough, homespun-clad farmers that surrounded him, if one might judge from his apparel and general demeanor.

A heavy gold watch-guard, from which depended a bunch of seals, crossed his waistcoat, and while with one hand holding a riding-whip, he daintily flecked a speck of dust from the tip of his well-polished boot, the other raised a glass of liquor from the bar. As he did so, a solitaire diamond ring flashed back the candlelight with a thousand scintillations. Among the frills of his linen shirt-front a magnificent cluster pin of the same jewels gleamed forth, exciting the wonder and admiration of a number of the men present.

At present his features were calm and expressionless, while his small gray eyes shone with a half-vacant air; but beneath all this a close observer would have seen something more. He would have pronounced the stolidity a mere mask, and would have seen that not a man present but was keenly scrutinized.

"Come, Dement," said Neil McGuire, turning toward this man. "Come, let's go," and the two men elbowed their way from the room.

The remainder, such as had not departed, continued to converse in low tones upon the subject of the strange voice. Poynter was carelessly leaning back against the counter, holding a glass in one hand, while he listened intently to the remarks, although not appearing to do so.

"It may be all right, Touter, but it is mighty queer, anyhow. And then who *is* this fellow? Do you know, does anybody know, except that he appears to have plenty of money, and calls himself Clay Poynter?" distinctly uttered a bold, free tone, and the speaker turned his head toward the person alluded to.

He was a somewhat remarkable-looking man, apparently five or six-and-twenty years of age. In form he was tall, and straight as an arrow, with a lithe suppleness in every movement, that, joined to his swarthy complexion, and long, straight black hair, in part confirmed the rumor that he had Indian blood in his veins.

"Ah, my dear Indian Polk," blandly interrupted Poynter, as he drew himself erect upon hearing these words. "You do not drink. Allow me to offer you a glass of brandy?" and with a lightning-like movement he hurled the heavy glass full at the head of the young man.

"But, quick as was the action, the missile was eluded by an adroit duck of the head, and Polk sprung forward with a fierce curse, lunging out with his clinched fist a fearful blow as he did so. The blow fell upon Poynter's half-averted cheek, tearing the skin as if cut with a knife; but not a quiver or a motion was the result of the blow.

Before the assailant could recover his balance, Poynter's left hand clutched his throat, and then the massive fist shot out, taking Polk full between the eyes, with such crushing force that he was hurled clear across the room, where he fell head-first in a senseless heap beneath the table.

Coolly wiping the blood-spots from his shirt-front with a handkerchief, Poynter turned to the bar without another glance at the fallen man, and called for a glass of brandy. Henderson promptly served it, at the same time whispering:

"You'd better look out, Mr. Poynter, fer 'Injun' hain't no baby, an' 'll hev y'ur blood fer this, ef so be he kin. He's a devil, shore!"

"Bah!" laughed Poynter, snapping his fingers. "I don't care *that* for him. If he crosses my path again, or lets me hear any more of his dirty hints, I'll hit him a square blow next, one that he'll not get over so easily as this one. But when he gets up, just give him my compliments, and tell him that if he relishes the specimen, there's plenty more of the same brand at his service," and so saying Clay Poynter left the room and vanished in the darkness, leaving those behind him still more puzzled at him than before.

CHAPTER II.

THE DOUBLE SHOT.

"WHAT can be keeping Nora, I wonder?" half-muttered a man, as he anxiously peered through the leafy screen before him, with a gesture of impatience.

A man, we said, and as he turns his head so that the sun's rays fall beneath the broad-brimmed slouched hat, we can see that it is Clay Poynter who is there awaiting the arrival of some person. Even had not his muttered exclamation revealed this fact, there was an eager, ardent tinge to his restlessness that would have betrayed his secret—would have told of an appointment with some one a little more than a mere friend.

A woman would have guessed that he was expecting a sweetheart, whom, for some reason, he could not visit openly, and she would have been right. He was awaiting a sweetheart, and her name was Nora McGuire.

Again Poynter peered through the bushes. He saw a small but neat vine-covered log house of only one story. Behind this and upon either hand spread the fields of young grain, now a level, waving sea of verdure, with strange forms and figures chasing each other, as the blades were bent by the fitful gusts of wind.

Behind this, again, rose the rugged mounds forming the "Wildcat Range," among whose more difficult recesses the "big game" still could be found, and it was rumored that yet more dangerous customers might there be met with—that many a wild scene of blood and crime those rock-crowned hills had witnessed.

But of this our friend took no heed, for he saw the object of his thoughts step from the cabin-door, and after a hasty glance around, trip lightly toward the spot where he was standing. Poynter pushed aside the screen of bushes, and half-emerged, but as if by a second thought he drew back with a muttered curse.

He had caught a glimpse of Neil McGuire's stalwart form passing from the field to the cabin, and for some reason best known to himself, did not wish those keen gray eyes to note his presence. The young girl now reached the screen of bushes, and, with one glance behind her, passed them, and then was tightly clasped in the strong arms of Poynter.

"For shame, Mr. Poynter, to surprise me in that way!" pouted the dainty lips, as Nora glided from the embrace.

"But, Nora, 'tis all your own fault, if I am obliged to surprise you, as you say," laughed the young man.

"And why so?" innocently queried the maiden, with the slightest possible toss of her pretty head.

"Well, pet, the fact is, I have a serious monomania that troubles a—"

"A what? Is it anything very dangerous?" asked Nora, with a startled air.

"That depends," he laughed again. "But, as I was saying, the disease is beyond my power to cure. It is, that whenever I see a dainty little rosebud mouth, like one that shall be nameless, I feel an irresistible desire to just stoop my head and see if it is as sweet as it looks!"

"Oh, you horrid creature! I thought you were sick, or something," pouted Nora, half-turning away.

"Now you're mad, and I've got something of importance to tell you."

"No, I am not mad; but you talk so queer at times that I can't understand you. You seem to light in making sport of me."

"I make sport of you? No, no, little one! I love you far too well for that. It is only my way! But come, take my arm and let's walk. I have something to say that cannot be postponed, and some one might interrupt us here," added Poynter.

"But can't you come to the house, Clay? It don't seem right for me to meet you in this manner," hesitated Nora.

"Your father is at home, and you know what he said the last time I called. If any one else had spoken to me in that way, Nora, he would—"

And then pausing abruptly for a moment, he added:

"But what has he told you about me, pet?"

"About you? why—" faltered the maiden.

"Come, Nora, it is better that I should hear it from you than him. No matter how harsh or unjust it may be, I shall not forget that he is your father."

"Oh, Clay, it was dreadful!"

"So bad as that? Well, my shoulders are broad and I can bear it. And it was—?"

"Must I tell?" she pleaded.

"Nora!"

"Well, then," with a sigh, "he said that he had heard you were connected with a gang of horse-thieves and counterfeiters; and although he had no positive proof against you, as yet, he forbade my speaking to you until he gave me leave."

"So-so!" bitterly exclaimed Poynter, half to himself. "My kind friend has not abandoned me yet." Then turning abruptly to Nora, he added: "And you believed this?"

"Clay!"

"Pardon, darling; I did not mean it," repentantly said Poynter. "No, I can trust you, if no one else."

And he clasped the little brown hand that had been laid upon his arm at her exclamation.

"I wish you would trust me; then, perhaps, I could tell better how to act," she said, looking up into his face, wistfully.

"And have I not? Well—did he tell you from where these hints came?"

"No, but I think—and yet again, I am puzzled," hesitated Nora.

"You think—?"

"That our strange visitor—this John Dement, he calls himself—is in some way mixed up with it. More than once I have accidentally overheard him and father speaking about you, but whenever they saw me, it would be dropped."

"The yellow-haired man that was with your father on Tuesday night?"

"Yes. But I may be wrong. At any rate, he has left us now."

"Left you, you say; and when?"

"Late yesterday afternoon. But it is only for a short time. I heard him tell father that he would return next week."

"Do you know where he went?"

"To Fort Leavenworth."

"Good! I will manage to have an interview with the gentleman; I must stop there myself."

"You stop there? Why Clay—!" exclaimed the maiden, in a startled tone.

"Yes; that is what I came to tell you. I must go to St. Louis upon business for a week or so. Indeed, I should have been upon the road before now, but I wished to see you first so that you would not be alarmed at my disappearance," returned Poynter, kindly.

The reply she was about to make was abruptly checked by the sound of approaching footsteps, and then the loud, clear call of:

"Nora, Nora child, where are you?"

"Oh, Clay, it is my father! He will kill me if he finds I am with you!"

"Never fear, darling, he will not hurt you," murmured Poynter, as he drew the trembling form closer to his side.

"No, no, Clay; but you—oh, leave me!"

"What, I run, and from one man?"

"Nora—I say, Nora; why don't you answer me?" impatiently called the voice, and the footsteps ceased, as if her father was listening.

"For my sake!" pleaded the maiden.

"For *your* sake—well," and with one fervent kiss, Clay Poynter vanished among the undergrowth.

"*Nora*—NORA!"

"Yes, father," she tremblingly answered.

"Oh, so here you are?" said Neil McGuire, as she entered the little glade. "Why didn't you speak before? Ha! who has been here with you?" he added, at the same time bending over the moist ground.

Nora could not reply, and then her father rose with an angry flush upon his face, and exclaimed, in a voice hoarse with passion:

"So, this is the way you obey me! Stop!" as he saw Nora about to speak, "do not add false-hood to disobedience—"

"Father, did I ever tell you a lie?" reproachfully asked Nora.

"Pardon, Nora, I did not mean that. But I was so angry at finding that you had been with that villain, Poynter, I forgot myself. See, those are his tracks. No other man wears such boots, around here."

"Well, I was with him, but he only came to bid me good-by."

"Good-by! Then he thinks it best to leave the country before Judge Lynch interviews him, the—"

"Hold, Mr. McGuire," slowly said Poynter, as he stepped forward and confronted the father. "Why should *I* fear Judge Lynch more than any other man?"

"Ah, why, indeed?" sneered McGuire. "Why was it that you left Kentucky so suddenly, and made such a short stop in Arkansas, if I may ask?"

"So *that* is your game, is it? Well, of this be assured, that after my return from St. Louis, I will show you such proofs of my innocence that you will beg pardon for your unjust suspicions."

"*After* your return!" echoed Neil, derisively.

"Father—father!" pleaded Norah, in terror, "come, let us go home; I'm afraid."

"Your daughter is right, Mr. McGuire," added Poynter, a little more coolly. "It will do no good for us to talk further. My explanations can wait."

"So I presume," curtly responded the other, then adding, "Come, child, let us go," and leading Nora by the hand, he left the glade.

For a few moments Poynter stood gazing abstractedly in the direction they had taken, and then arousing himself, with a little laugh, turned upon his heel and walked briskly along a faintly-defined trail.

After crossing a slight rise and down the valley once more, Poynter came in view of his own house—for that time and section, a perfect palace, a two-story frame, weather-boarded, and painted a neat cream-color. Why he had built this, when he was not at home one-tenth of his time, was a great puzzle to his neighbors, and many a siege of cross-questioning had old aunty Eunice to undergo.

Questions as to who her young master really was, if wealthy, and his reasons for making such frequent journeys; why he had not got married, and countless others, of equal importance. But the old negress knew how to keep a close tongue in her head, or to talk a great deal without saying anything; so that when her visitors left they were forced to acknowledge that they knew as much as they did before—and not much more.

Clay Poynter strode rapidly along, but h thoughts were not upon what he was doing; was thinking of Nora McGuire. His head w bent forward, but he did not heed where stepped, and with a sharp cry of surprise he fe headlong, his foot having caught against a ro or stub.

It is wonderful upon what slight points man's life hinges; and Poynter had an instan of this fact furnished him at the same momen Simultaneous with his cry, a double repo echoed upon the air, and his hat fluttered fro his head, and a sharp, tingling sensation in h shoulder told him that he was shot.

"Hurray, Bart, he's a goner!" shouted a voi that the fallen man had no difficulty in reco nizing.

"Bet ye! But it's halfers, mind ye no Polk!" and at the same time two men broke o from the bushes, and hastened toward their i tended victim.

Poynter could see them plainly, and immed ately recognized them to be Barton Clowry a Polk Redlaw, the former a drunken, worthle scoundrel, that would lie, steal, fight and drin day in and day out. He had a fit-looking pers for a partner, owing to the blow dealt Polk Re law by Poynter, at the "Twin Sycamores that had inflamed his entire face dreadfully.

All this he saw at a glance, and when the tw would-be murderers had crossed half the inte vening space, Poynter leaped to his feet with hoarse cry, and as his right arm straighten out, the sun's rays flashed upon the polished t of a revolver. At the report, Clowry gav convulsive spring, and then fell upon his dead.

"Now, you dirty, mongrel cur, it is y turn!" yelled Poynter as he again cocked weapon.

It was discharged, but Polk had caught t motion, and throwing himself flat upon ground, the missile hissed harmlessly above head. But ere he could arise, Poynter lea forward and dealt him a fearful kick upor side of his head, that hurled him forward t his length, sprawling among the bushes, wh he lay perfectly limp and motionless.

His enemy stooped over him and felt c body, then arising, he muttered·

"Dead as the other! Well, it munition saved, at any rate. It is a bad though, but it was either I or them, and t *would* have it!" he muttered, as he returne where his hat lay, brushing the dust from garments.

"New hat spoiled—item first; bullet-hol shoulder, another. Well, I don't know b they are both paid for, now, as it turn. Confound the thing! how it does smar Eunice must bind it up, and then I must go and tell the neighbors," he mus proceeded toward the house.

"Curse the luck! More delay jus should be at work; and if I was not ver before, will this mend matters any?

they were such dirty hounds, or it might go hard with me. And then these Vigilantes—"

"Lord 'a' massy! Marse Clay," cried a husky, wheezing voice, as a negro woman came waddling from around the house. "Is you done kilt, honey?"

"Not quite, aunty," laughed Poynter. "But I might have been. Come," he added, entering the building, "get some rags and bind up my shoulder."

"'Clar' to goodness, honey, chile, I was e'ena'most skeered to deaf, I jest was, now," chattered Aunt Eunice, as she bustled around her patient. "I jest done went to de do' to look ef you was a-comin', w'en I see'd dem 'ar funnelly fellers a-shootin', an' den you falled down, an' I t'ought you's done dead fo' suah!"

"Well, why didn't you come and help me?"

"'Deed I was jest a-gwine, honey, so I was. I runned to de kitchen, an' got dis yere," holding up a huge basting-fork, "'nd w'en I got out ag'in, dar you was, big's life. "Pear's like, I'd a-drapped, I's so 'mazin' glad. Bress ye, honey, dear, ef dem 'ar Pharoasters 'd 'a' killed you, I'd a—jest would, so dar!" spluttered the old woman, throwing her arms around Clay, and jumping up and down as she hugged him.

"Easy—easy, aunty; you hurt my arm," laughed Poynter, as he released himself, and then sunk into a chair, feeling faint from excitement and loss of blood.

"Jest looky! w'at a funnelly ole goose I is! But I's so glad, Marse Clay, dat it 'pears like I'll go clean crazy."

"I think that if you'd get me some brandy or a cup of coffee, it would be a more sensible idea, Aunt Eunice."

"Dar 'tis ag'in! Might 'a' knowed dat. But you jest sot still, honey, 'nd I'll git you it," and she trotted out of the room with an alacrity that made the entire house jar beneath her weight, while Poynter bowed his head upon the table.

CHAPTER III.
"JUDGE LYNCH."

AFTER drinking the coffee prepared by Aunt Eunice, Poynter started toward the door with the intention of mounting his horse and giving information to his neighbors concerning the tragedy, but his limbs trembled and his head reeled, forcing him to catch at the door-post in order to keep from falling. A strange spell of weakness seized him, and but for the strong arm of his servant, who supported him to a chair, he would have sunk to the floor.

"Fix my bed, aunty; I guess I'll lie down for a moment. I must have bled far more than I thought. And just at the time when I should be most active, too!" he muttered, half uneasily, as the old woman departed upon her errand.

In a few moments he was lying down upon the bed, and dismissed Aunt Eunice about her work. He sank into a heavy slumber, that lasted until late in the afternoon, when he was hastily aroused by his servant, who appeared to be terribly alarmed at something.

"Well, what is up, Eunice? You look as if you'd seen the ghost of your grandfather."

"Lor', ef 'twas on'y jest a ghos', 'pears like I'd glad!" cried the old woman, anxiously.

"Bress you, honey, dar's a right smart chance o' dem ar' critter-back fellers out yander, all a-holdin' guns an' sich like, w'at tole me was you hyar? Den I tole dem, I dunno; 'spect you done gwine away; 'cause I didn't know w'at dey wanted, an' didn't know mebbe you'd want to hide. Den a gre't big feller, no 'count w'ite trash, he said, 'G'long, dar, you 'sense o' midnight you, an' tell him to show hisse'f, or I brow de whull top o' y'ur head offen you!' Den I say, 'Git out, you dirty w'ite nigger'—" spluttered the woman, when Poynter, who had pulled on his boots and coat, interrupted her by asking:

"Armed horsemen, you say; did you know any of them?"

"'Deed I did so, honey. Dar's ol' Marse Reeves, 'n' Brooks 'nd dat ar' Injun feller—" began Eunice.

"What! not Polk Redlaw?"

"'Deed, fo' suah, Marse Clay, honey," persisted Eunice. "I knowed de dirty nigger, dough his face is all bloody, an' red like a b'iled beet."

Poynter did not reply, but proceeded hastily through the house and out upon the front stoop, where his appearance was hailed with an exultant shout from the crowd of armed men that filled the dooryard.

"There he is—arrest him! I charge him with murder!" cried out a loud voice, a little upon one side.

"Ah! you there, mongrel cur?" scornfully cried the accused, with a look of contempt. "I thought I had finished you for good."

"See, he acknowledges it!" foamed Polk Redlaw; "I call you all to witness—"

"Dry up y'ur yaup," muttered one of his neighbors, giving Redlaw a shove that nearly sent him to the ground head-foremost.

"Curse you, Jack Fyffe!" snarled Polk, leaping at the man with a gleaming knife in his hand, "I'll cut your heart out!"

"So!" coolly exclaimed the burly fellow, dodging aside and dealing the battered head of his assailant a deftly-planted blow that brought him to grass. "'Pears like 'sif y'ur ockyputt was a football, sorter."

"Stop your squabbling there," called out Neil McGuire, sternly. "The first one that creates a disturbance while I lead them, will be put under arrest. Young man," he added, turning to Poynter, who stood calmly scrutinizing the assembly before him, "I regret it for your sake, but I must arrest you," at the same time ascending the steps and placing his hand upon Poynter's shoulder.

"Arrest me!" said the young man, shaking off the grasp and retreating a step. "And for what?"

A yell went up from the crowd; among the cries were fearful words—those of *robbery* and *murder!*

"You hear?" significantly returned McGuire.

"I do; but even supposing those terms applied to me, what right have *you* to take the office of justice upon yourself?"

"What right? That of the people—of honest men! The right that justifies a man in killing a snake, or ridding the community of a scourge. We are *Vigilantes*—did you ever hear of them before—in Kentucky, for instance?" sternly replied Neil, with a biting sneer upon the last question.

"Ah!"

It was only one word, but it comprised a world of bitterness—one might almost say of anguish and despair. It seemed as if a dreadful blow had been stricken him, and for a moment he bowed his head beneath it; but only for a moment. Then he was as cool and as proud as before.

"Very well. I suppose I am your prisoner?"

"You are."

"Aunt Eunice, don't be alarmed, I will return soon. Then turning to McGuire, he added, "I presume I will have a fair trial?"

"We are not murderers—only the ministers of justice," was the stern reply.

"Then, aunty, when I send for you, come. I may need your evidence."

"'Deed, Marse Clay, honey," sobbed the old woman, pressing forward, "I's gwine along too."

"No, you cannot; at least just now. Remain here until I send." Then to the leader of the Vigilantes. "Well, sir, I am ready!"

"Your horse?"

"Is in the stable—my bay, I mean. The other was stolen."

"Stolen?"

"I told you as much at the meeting."

"Well, Crane, bring him out," and then McGuire drew aside with two men, to whom he appeared giving some instructions, in a low, guarded voice.

The horse of the prisoner was brought forth, and when he had mounted, they filed from the dooryard, and closing up around their captive rode away, with the exception of the two men spoken to by McGuire, who soon after entered the building.

The little cavalcade proceeded at a rapid trot toward the "Twin Sycamores," while the curious, half-affrighted gazes that followed them from each house as they passed, told that a rumor of their mission had spread like wildfire.

Poynter's mind was not idle, and he realized that his liberty, if not life, was in jeopardy; and that, too, when freedom was most inestimable. He did not know what charges would be brought against him; but it was evident that the hint given by Neil McGuire regarding the Kentucky Vigilantes troubled his mind not a little.

In a few minutes the party drew rein in front of the "Twin Sycamores"—so named from the two gigantic trees of that species growing upon either side of the door—where stood "Honest Jim." The captain whispered a few words in his ear.

"Wal, ef you wish it; thar's nobody thar." Then, as he drew nearer to Poynter, he added in a kind tone: "Lord love you, squar', I'm sorry —dog-goned sorry to see you hyar. It's rough lines fer a fine young feller like you to be 'rested on sech a charge!"

"Thank you, Henderson," cordially replied Poynter, as he clasped the little man's hand warmly. "It is rough, especially when you are innocent."

"Be—now don't git mad, Mr. Poynter, 'cause I mean well—be you innercent?" anxiously asked Henderson.

"Of anything unlawful or mean, I am. But as I don't know what charges are laid against me, I can say no more."

"They say you be one of these horse-thieves an' counterfeiters!" whispered the landlord.

"Then they lie!" angrily replied Poynter.

"An' wuss, a heap wusser'n that. They say you *murdered*—"

"No conversing with the prisoner, there, Jim Henderson," interrupted the leader, as he emerged from the house.

"I was jest a—"

"No matter. Come. The long-room is ready, and to spare time we will try the prisoner at once," added McGuire, as he motioned his men to enter.

The "long-room" was that in which we saw the first meeting of the Vigilantes, and as all entered, the door was closed and securely bolted, thus guarding against any intrusion. The long table was pushed along until it touched the further end of the wall, and upon this a single chair was placed. Then a similar one was stood near the other extremity for the prisoner's use.

"Now, gentlemen," said Neil McGuire, "we will vote for a judge to try the case."

By universal acclamation he was elected, and at once took his seat, when Poynter was directed to assume his position. After some few objections by the prisoner, a jury was chosen and ranged alongside the judge, who then spoke:

"You know the task that is before you, and the sooner it is over the better. We will—"

"One moment, Mr. McGuire—or I presume I should say *your Honor*," interrupted Poynter, with an ironical bow. "You call this a trial, but is it not altogether one-sided? Here I am arrested, for what I know not; already treated like a felon. Is *this* your idea of justice?"

"You speak warmly, Mr. Poynter—"

"And why not? You are all leagued against me, and so far as I can see, do not intend giving me a chance to clear myself from any charge you may bring against me. If I am to be tried, I demand it shall be according to law, and that I have counsel; that I am informed what crime I am accused of, and allowed time to procure witnesses!" hotly exclaimed the prisoner.

"You shall have full justice, but we have no need for lawyers here. The truth alone shall acquit or condemn you. You can defend yourself, and if any witnesses are necessary they shall be sent for. If you are shown to be innocent, then any reparation you demand shall be given, but if guilty, by the God that made me, you shall swing for it, if I have to draw the rope myself!"

"One would think I was already condemned, by the way you speak; but go on. What are your charges?"

"Polk Redlaw!"

"Here!"

"Your turn first. Tell us your story. But briefly and to the point," ordered the "judge."

"Well, I heard the prisoner was suspected—"

"Never mind that now, but come to your charge first."

"Then I charge him with murdering Barton Clowry, and nearly killing me!" snarled the witness.

"You hear, prisoner; guilty or not guilty?"

"That I killed Clowry, and tried to serve that mongrel the same, I admit; but it was in self-defense, not *murder*," promptly replied Poynter.

"He lies—"

"Silence! Mr. Redlaw, no abuse if you please. State your case," ordered McGuire.

"Well, as I was saying, I, together with Barton Clowry, was ordered to scout around the house of the prisoner, and as soon as he returned to inform the band so that they could arrest him without his having a chance to escape, as he would had they hunted him with the whole league. We concealed ourselves by the side of the road, and were talking together to pass away the time, when I heard a pistol-shot, and Bart fell dead over into my lap.

"Before I could get up I saw the prisoner come running toward us, and aiming at me he fired again, but missed. Then he struck me with his revolver, knocking me back as I tried to get up; then kicked and pounded me upon the head until he thought I was dead.

"I was only stunned, however, and when I came to, I managed to crawl away, and finding the Vigilantes I told them my story. You were notified, and going with us, you know the rest," concluded Polk; his speech being followed by a deep, fierce murmur that told how fully his apparently frank and truthful story had been believed.

"Mr. McGuire, and you, gentlemen," exclaimed Poynter, springing to his feet, but as the position in which he was placed would not allow him to stand erect, he sunk back into the chair. "Gentlemen! Every word that mongrel has said is a base, foul lie! and if you will send for my housekeeper, you will see that it is so.

"I was walking peaceably along the lane toward my house, when two shots were fired at me from an ambush. See; here is the mark of one in my hat, and if you examine my left shoulder you can see the trace left by the other.

"Did he say any thing about shooting at me? You, Mr. McGuire, know that I was not wounded this forenoon when I saw you. I admit shooting Clowry, but it was in self-defense. Does it look reasonable, or even possible, that *had* I done as this scoundrel states, I would have returned to the house to lie down and sleep for hours? Would I not have mounted and fled?"

"There is reason in what you say," uttered the judge. "But you said you had proof; did she witness the affair?"

"Yes; my negro housekeeper saw it all."

"Fox, you and Bowers go and bring her here immediately," ordered he leader. Then turning toward Polk Redlaw, he added, slowly: "Well, you hear what *he* says? Mind how you reply, for it is no light thing to wrongfully accuse a man of such a crime."

"I have told you the truth and nothing else," sullenly replied the accuser. "He has had plenty of time to trump up a yarn and teach his wench what to say. A white man's word ought to be good against a nigger's, any day."

"If true, it will be."

At this point the proceedings were interrupted by the entrance of the two messengers and aunt Eunice, whom they had met almost at the door —she having followed her master with the best speed her unwieldy body was capable of.

We need not follow her evidence as it is already known, and confirmed Poynter's story. But as the prisoner glanced around the room, he was surprised to note the still dark and vindictive faces of the Vigilantes, who appeared anything but convinced. Then he spoke, addressing the judge:

"Well, sir, what is your decision?"

"On this score you are fully acquitted; but—"

"'On *this* charge!' Are there any more, then?"

"Two others. Passing counterfeit money, and *murder*."

"Murder!"

"Yes; the murder of John Dement!"

CHAPTER IV.

THE CRY FOR BLOOD!

CLAY POYNTER sat as if perfectly astounded at these words; then, as he recovered from the shock and glanced around him, he could read in the faces of all that he was deemed guilty of this black deed. Only one face but wore this look; one face, and that belonged to Aunt Eunice.

She stood with her hands thrown up, her eyes rolling wildly, while her capacious mouth opened and shut by jerks, as if she was trying to speak. Then with an explosive snort, she spluttered:

"Well, ef you hain't jest de biggest liar on top o' dis yere airth, den I don't know nuffin! Mars'r Clay—*my* chile—do dat ar'? *He*—w'y, you cussed funnelly fools—Lord 'a' massy, 'pears like I's gwine to bu'st, 'deed it does!"

"Take her out, some of you," angrily ordered the judge.

"Yes, aunty, you'd better go now," interposed Poynter. "It's all a mistake like the other one, and will be over soon."

He had not time to say more, for the old negress was unceremoniously hustled out of the "court-room," and the door again barred. Then the proceedings were resumed. Upon the charge of passing counterfeit money, Jim Henderson testified that the prisoner had given him a base five-dollar coin in payment of his score upon the night of the first meeting, receiving change in good silver.

Was positive of the fact, because it was the only coin of that denomination he had received that day. Upon this Poynter admitted that he might have done so, unknowing that the coin was spurious, and instanced several cases of his being served the same way, owing to the vast amount of counterfeit money then in circulation.

"Jonathan Green!" called out the judge, acting as crier.

"Hyar I be!" grunted a coarse voice, as a man elbowed his way through the crowd toward the open space reserved for witnesses.

He was a short, squat-built, villainous-looking fellow of perhaps forty years, although strong drink and excesses may have contributed several of them. He cast a sidelong, sneaking glance at Poynter, and then suddenly averted his head.

The prisoner made a sudden motion as if about

to speak, but then sunk back once more, his eyes steadily fixed upon Green's face.

This action was not unnoted by the jurors, and more than one thought they could discern a shudder pass over his form, as he darted a peculiar look at the witness. Green was sworn, and proceeded to give in his testimony.

"Yas, 'ir, I'll tell ye the hull truth, jist es straight es a dogwood, ef on'y you'll promus 'at no harm 'll come arter it. He's mighty rambunctious, he is, when his mad's up."

"Never you mind about that, sir," impatiently said McGuire, "but give in your testimony."

"Wal, ef I must, why, so be it I've knowed the pris'ner thar a consid'able spell, ef not longer. Me 'n' him usen to be gre't fri'nds an' pardners like, back to ol' Kaintuck—"

"Gentlemen, is this scoundrelly liar brought here to swear away my life? As I live, I have never seen the fellow half a dozen times; I didn't even know his name, beyond that of 'Lying Jack,' and never spoke a word to him in my life!" exclaimed the prisoner, hotly.

"Silence!" ordered the judge.

"Hyar's my hat," put in Green, extending the rag that answered that purpose, with a comical leer. "I never told a bigger lie 'n' that in my life!"

"Witness, you will go on with your evidence, or, by all that's good, I'll give you a taste of hickory oil!" thundered the judge.

"Jes' so! But, es I war sayin', I knowed 'im in ol' Kaintuck jist afore he war driv' away by the Vigilantes—"

"For what reason?" asked one of the jurors.

"I don't know. Mebbe 'twas 'cause he scattered too much o' the *queer*, mebbe 'twasn't," returned the witness, significantly. "Anyhow, he left, an' then I nixt see'd him hyar. One day —mebbe two weeks gone by—he come to me an' says, says he, 'Green, my fri'nd, what you doin', anyhow?' 'Oh, jist sorter sloshin' round, like,' says I.

"Then arter a w'ile he said he could put me in a leetle way to make money, ef I'd no 'bjection. He said he's in the ol' business, an' wanted me to take holt and try to sell the 'queer,' offerin' to let me hev it fer fifteen dollars a hundred, till I sorter got started, an' found rig'lar customers. I pertended to be all-fired glad, an' he guv me one hundred dollars on tick."

"But why didn't you tell of this before?" demanded the judge.

"An' git sarved like Bart Clowry! Who was I to go to, ontel I hearn thet you-'uns was on the trail? Es soon's I knowed thet, I come an' told you, didn't I?"

"Have you any of the money with you?"

"Yas," replied the witness, drawing a small package from his bootleg. "Hyar it is. I kep' it hid till to-day, 'cause ef it 'd 'a' bin found on me afore, the fellers mought 'a' thunk I's one o' them 'ar fellers."

The money, all in five-dollar coins, was passed to the jurors who, after a careful examination, pronounced it to be counterfeit. Surely, the case began to look black for the prisoner, but he still maintained a haughty look upon his pale, handsome features, while his eye flashed back the angry glances that were cast at him from all sides.

"That is all the evidence upon the first charge, I believe," spoke McGuire, but he was interrupted by a voice from the crowd:

"Begging pardon, judge, but there's more yet," and the speaker, one of the two men who had remained behind at the prisoner's house, came forward, and held up a pair of dies made for coining half-eagles. "These toys were found at the house concealed in the chimney-jamb."

Amidst the greatest excitement, Frank Dalton was sworn, and deposed to this effect. He and Sam Gibson had made a search of the premises after Poynter's capture. After a time they had found the dies, concealed as stated; and a small package of newly-coined money, tied up in an old rag at the bottom of the prisoner's trunk, and thinking they would be needed as evidence, had brought them away.

Samuel Gibson, who was a well-known and respected farmer, fully corroborated Dalton's statement as to the discovery, and when he concluded, any slight doubt that might have been entertained as to the prisoner's guilt, was entirely dispelled.

The hoarse murmur that filled the room began to increase in volume, and dark, deadly hints could be distinguished. Hints that soon grew into open threats, calling for a conviction—a conviction that would be equivalent to *death*.

Still the prisoner did not quail or tremble. He even drew himself up with a bolder defiance, and not one man of them all but turned their eyes away from his when their gaze met.

"Peace, gentlemen," spoke McGuire, half arising—the ceiling would allow no more—and waving his hand to command silence. "All in good time. There is yet another charge upon which he must be tried. If justice pauses, it will none the less be carried out.

"Wesley Sprowl!" he called out, once order was restored.

A little weasel-faced man approached the stand for witnesses. His form was bowed and emaciated, as if from some recent severe illness, and a hectic cough appeared to trouble him exceedingly, as he gave in his evidence, frequently causing him to pause and lean heavily against the table for support.

As soon as he had partially regained his breath, the judge ordered him to proceed with his testimony, after being duly sworn. But his first words were lost to the majority of the assembly, owing to his low tone; but he soon gathered strength, and every word was uttered with a clear distinctness, that from its deliberation, every sentence appeared to be carefully weighed before being spoken.

"I know the prisoner well, partly because he is not a common-looking man, but more so from feeling a friendly interest in him. He has often been at my house, and when I was nearly dead with the chills, and had no money, he brought me some quinine that cured me. I tell you this so that you may see how impossible it would be for me to mistake another for him.

"I was feeling quite unwell all day yesterday, and could not sleep any last night from that cause. Many of you know that I have lines constantly set in the river, by night as well as by day. Somehow my mind got to dwelling upon them, and I could not banish a fancy that occurred to me, of there being a great big catfish upon one of the lines.

"At length I became so convinced that it was so, I dressed, and went out toward the river. Somehow I didn't think of taking any weapon with me, my mind was so full of the big fish.

"Well, I struck into the road at the cornfield, and then, as the easiest way, I followed the road, intending to strike the branch where a plain trail leads to the river. But, just as I got to the old 'Ivy Elm,' I heard loud voices coming directly toward me.

"So I slipped behind the tree to let them pass, for in these rough times you don't know who you might meet, and although I hadn't anything worth stealing, it wouldn't be the first man who'd been rubbed out just for fun. But they were long in coming up, and appeared to stop twice, talking in loud and, as I thought, angry tones, before they paused exactly in front of me.

"By reaching out my arm I could have touched the largest man, they were that close; and by the voice I thought I could recognize the prisoner. I was so frightened that I could only distinguish one sentence spoken by the latter: '*And you won't let that Kentucky scrape drop?*'

"Those were his exact words, and the other man answered no, that he would tell all.

"Then I saw the larger one draw back his right hand, and could distinguish the gleam of a knife. The same moment, the other man stumbled and fell, muttering with a groan that he was killed. Twice more he was stabbed, and then the murderer appeared to be searching his body.

"I could see him take something white from an inner pocket and put it into his breast, but the shadow was so dense that I could not tell what it was, nor yet see their features plain enough to be sure of their identity. But then, with a curse, the murderer struck a match, and holding it close to the body, bent down his own head.

"He was unfastening something from his victim's shirt-bosom that gleamed and sparkled in the light like lightning-bugs. The match lasted only a moment, but that was long enough for me to distinguish plainly the features of both men.

"The murdered one was the sandy-complexioned man that has been staying with Mr. McGuire, and the other was—"

Here the witness faltered for a moment.

"And the other?" demanded the judge.

"*The murderer was the prisoner, Clay Poynter!*"

A deep, hoarse cry of rage and fury ran around the crowd of spectators, but far above it roared the clear, metallic tones of the accused:

"It is false, every word—false as h—l!"

In vain the judge shouted for order; his call was unheeded. The crowd swayed to and fro for a moment, and then rushed forward, as one man, to seize upon the prisoner.

But Neil McGuire ran along the table and stood beside Poynter, with a cocked revolver in his hand. The next instant, obedient to his call, the jurors gathered around, similarly armed. Then McGuire spoke, in a tone that overpowered the tumult:

"Stand back—back with you! By the God that made me, if one of you dare to lay a hand on the prisoner, I will spatter the wall with your brains!"

"Hang the murderer—burn him!" roared the crowd.

"Once more, I say, stand back!" yelled the judge, threatening the foremost with his pistol. "Is he not in our power?"

In a few moments order was restored, the judge and jurors resuming their seats, while Wesley Sprowl continued his story:

"I nearly fell, from horror and astonishment, when I saw who the murderer was, but managed to keep still. If you ask why I didn't confront him, or attempt to avenge John Dement, I say, look at us both. He, with ten times my strength, and fully armed, while I was barely able to walk, and without a single weapon.

"After a bit, the murderer took up the body in his arms and carried it to the river, where I heard a splash as if it had been cast into the water. I dared not stay longer, and stepping into the road, where I knew he could not hear my footsteps in the soft dirt, was about to run when something bright caught my eye. I snatched it up and then ran as fast as I could to the house, where I hid the article in the bed.

"In the morning I was down with a hard shake, and it was nearly noon before I could get up. But then I came over here, and knowing the head men of the league, I told what I knew about the affair. What happened since, you all know."

"But the thing that you found—what was it?"

"I have it here—see!" and after unwrapping a small parcel, he elevated his hand.

In it was a piece of jewelry. *It was the diamond cluster-pin lately worn by John Dement!*

There was no uproar now. A deadly calm had settled upon the assembly. A calm that spoke plainer than words or oaths.

It spoke of death.

"Gentlemen," slowly said the judge, "I need not ask if this pin is recognized; we all know it. And it shows that a bloody, dastardly deed has been committed. The verbal evidence is all given in; but still we must not be rash. Let us first search the river for the body, so that there may be no doubt. It is too late now to conclude to-night. Besides, the daylight is better. It will show that we are not ashamed of our actions."

"And what shall we do with the murderer?" interrupted one of the jurors.

"We can guard him until to-morrow. This room is safe, especially as he will be bound."

"Well, he is guilty of counterfeiting, anyhow, and for that we condemn him to receive one hundred lashes upon the bare back. It would be more but for the other charge."

"Yes, and to-night! We won't go home without some fun," interrupted one of the spectators.

"I protest!" cried McGuire. "Let him suffer but one punishment. Don't let's act like savages."

"No, no," yelled the crowd; "do it now, or else we'll finish up the job off-hand."

The excitement now grew intense; weapons were freely drawn and brandished, and although the judge stood over the prisoner with ready revolver, he was unsupported. The jurors had gone with the majority.

"Better give in, judge," called out the juror who had pronounced the sentence. "You see you can do no good, and will only get hurt. You have done all one man can do, but the boys are determined, even if costs a dozen lives."

"Don't get yourself into trouble upon my account, Mr. McGuire," exclaimed the prisoner. "These devils want blood, and it may as well come now as to-morrow. Besides," and here he lowered his tone, "remember your—family."

CHAPTER V.
BORDER LAW.

"GENTLEMEN!" said the judge, after a moment's pause, "if you persist in this outrage, I wash my hands of both it and you, from this moment. You can choose another judge, and another leader, for I shall act no longer as either. I thought you were men, not savages."

"What matter?" called out several voices, "he is not the only man that lives. Let him slide, and out with the prisoner."

The crowd surged forward and surrounded the table, yelling and growling like wild beasts. For a moment it seemed as if Poynter meditated resistance, as he drew himself up and grasped the back of his chair, but if such was his intention, it was changed.

A dozen hands lifted him to the floor, where he was securely bound, hand and foot—as he had been until now entirely free so far as bonds were concerned. Then he was lifted bodily upon their shoulders, each man appearing eager to be one of his bearers. In this manner he was conveyed from the room, followed by the hooting, yelling crowd; leaving but one man behind —Neil McGuire.

To say that the prisoner was not alarmed, would perhaps be wrong, but he showed no outward sign of being so.

Suddenly Poynter gave a convulsive start. It seemed to him he had heard, above the din, some words spoken in a friendly tone—words of hope.

"Keep a stiff upper lip, square. *We'll git you cl'ar afore day!*"

These were the words he had, or thought he had heard, close to his ear, and turned his eyes wonderingly to that point. He could distinguish the rough features of Jack Fyffe, the man who had knocked Polk Redlaw down at the time of arrest.

But he had no time for a question, or anything beyond seeing that Fyffe supported his right shoulder; for the next moment he was rudely cast down at the foot of one of the gigantic sycamores, beside the outer door. The tumult was horrible, and for a time nothing was done, each man issuing orders, but no one appearing to care about executing them.

"Jim Henderson!" yelled Polk Redlaw, who now took a decided lead with the brutalized crowd, "fetch out some cords, rope or something, quick!"

"Quick y'urself, Injun Polk," growled the little host. "I hain't y'ur nigger. Y'u're black enough to wait on y'urself!"

"Curses on you, you little hop-toad!" foamed Polk. "Call me that again, and I'll blow a hole through you big enough to kick a dog through!"

"Ef so be you know when y'ur well off, Mr. White Man, es-quire," coolly returned Jim, drawing his revolver; "you'll not buck ag'in' me. Others may be as quick on the trigger as you be, if not more so."

"Don't get to fighting among yourselves," interrupted Reeves, with a series of oaths. "We've enough to do now. Here's a couple of halters that'll answer bully."

But during this byplay, Clay Poynter had received considerable encouragement from Jack Fyffe, who still crouched over him, apparently to prevent his arising.

"Don't gi'n up, straunger," he had whispered. "We'll hev you free afore long."

"Who are you, and what do you mean?" asked Poynter.

"You'll see. I've sent arter the boys, an' ef nothin' happins, they'll be hyar in three hours. But you'll hev to take the hidin', though. We hain't strong enough to prevent th*it*."

Nothing more was said, for Redlaw and Reeves pressed forward, and with several brutal kicks from the mongrel, Poynter was lifted up and his arms unbound, two men clinging to each as though they anticipated an attempt at escape. But if so, they were disappointed.

The prisoner knew that it would be followed by certain death.

He was drawn up to the tree, his arms outstretched to their utmost extent, and then his wrists were connected by the halters, another securing his body. By this time the men who had been dispatched after the instruments of torture returned bearing their hands full of long, lithe hickory rods.

And then the torture began. The supple rods whistled through the air, and paused with a hissing crack; the gore started out as the tender skin was torn and lacerated. But although the pain and agony must have been fearful, as the punishment proceeded, not a groan or an uneven breath proclaimed the fact.

Polk Redlaw, Jonathan Green and Alfred Wigan plied the rods, and as may be supposed, they did not spare their strength. But severe as were their blows, they failed in drawing a single manifestation of pain from the prisoner, however slight. And then the one hundred lashes were counted, fairly.

The prisoner was let down from his position, and Jack Fyffe helped him to adjust his garments, managing to whisper a cheering word without being overheard by the mob. Then Poynter spoke, not a tremor or quaver betraying what he had suffered from the fearful ordeal, in his voice:

"You three devils, mark my words. If you are alive one week from to-day, I give you leave to play this game over again."

"We will live to see you dance on nothing, anyhow," sneered the mongrel.

"That's enough for to-night," interrupted Henry Reeves, the juror who had so suddenly taken a leading part in the proceedings, pressing forward and laying his hand upon Poynter's shoulder. "Come, you will stay in the 'long-room' to-night, and to prevent you from sleeping uneasily, I will add that you will be hung to-morrow, for murder."

"Thank you for nothing!" curtly replied the prisoner. "I have you to thank for this favor, and look you, it's a debt that will be paid; yes, paid, and with compound interest added," said Poynter.

"Oh, I'll credit you," laughed Reeves. "I always was accommodating. But in with you," he added, giving him a rude shove as they entered the room.

Poynter would have fallen had not he been caught by Jack Fyffe, who whispered:

"Ef you hyar a rumpus outside, don't be 'larmed, 'cause it'll on'y be fri'nds. Mind an' keep awake."

A pressure of the hand told that Poynter understood his meaning, and then, after being bound, the prisoner was left alone in the room. Some half a dozen guards were posted around the building, with instructions to shoot him if he attempted an escape; and then the Vigilantes separated, each man wending his way homeward.

The guards were in high glee, and having each one managed to procure a flask of liquor from the obliging host, determined to enjoy their watch to the best of their ability.

They were gathered in couples upon either side of the building, thus surrounding the place and preventing either egress or ingress without their knowledge. They little dreamed of the fate that awaited them.

Perhaps an hour after the dispersal, a band of horsemen drew rein at a half-mile from the little hamlet, on the outer edge of which stood the "Twin Sycamores," and dismounting, threw themselves upon the ground, while one of their number stole away on foot. He soon drew near the tavern, and sinking flat upon his stomach, began cautiously circling the building.

He could approach near enough, thanks to the darkness, to distinguish the mutterings of the guards—thus learning their exact number and position. He counted six, and thought it was all, but he overlooked Polk Redlaw, who had fallen into a doze, lying close to the wall, so that he seemed to form a portion of it.

Had he been awake he could not have helped observing the spy, who, thinking that end of the house unguarded, passed close by him. Muttering his surprise, the man crept away from the tavern, and once beyond ear-shot, rose to his feet and sped rapidly away to where he had left his companions.

When near them he muttered the howl of the yellow wolf and upon the signal being answered, boldly advanced and stood before the band. One, a tall, herculean man, stepped forward and whispered:

"Well, Fyffe, what luck?"

"It's all hunky," replied Jack, for it was indeed he, "an' a easy job. On'y six fellers, an' they half drunk, ef not more so," and then he clearly described the position each man occupied.

"Now, comrades," added he who appeared to be the leader, "you know what we are after. A friend, and one of us, is in danger. Our law says that we must assist each other, and now is the time. You have heard what Fyffe says. These men must be secured without being harmed if possible, but if they cut up rough, why a knife is the best remedy. The less blood shed, the better, for this section is getting uncomfortably hot already. You understand me?"

A murmur of general assent; then he added:

"We will ride to the edge of the timber, and then leave the horses. We must take them by surprise; and mind you, when once we have got our friend, quick's the word, for we will have the Vigilantes after us, hot-footed."

In a few moments the designated point of woods was reached, and dismounting, the hor es were secured; after which the band stealthily proceeded toward the tavern, using every precaution to avoid discovery. Then four men crept toward each of the sides where the double guard were posted.

The remainder held themselves in readiness to rush forward, in case their comrades should need any help. Four of the men were secured without any noise, other than a slight scuffle, but the other party were not so fortunate.

One of the guards caught a glimpse of the rescuers, and hailed them. The answer was an instant rush, at which the guard fired a shot that brought one of his assailants to the ground.

But ne never fired another, for a long knife was plunged downward, the steel gritting as it severed his breast-bone, and with one faint gurgle, Alfred Wigan was a dead man.

CHAPTER VI.
THE HUMAN BLOODHOUND.

AT the first report, Polk Redlaw sprung to his feet, with all the Indian instincts of his nature fully aroused. He caught a glimpse of the main body rushing forward, and not knowing who they were, he dropped to the ground and glided to a safe distance, but from whence he could still see those out in the open ground.

At first he thought it was the Vigilance Committee returned to finish up their work, but he was not certain, and deeming discretion the better course, determined to keep shady until he knew what card to play. If a rescue, he resolved to dog them wherever they might go, for his hatred of Poynter could only be assuaged by the latter's death.

When the double tragedy was over, and the other guards secured, the band rushed forward and forcibly burst in the door of the tavern; and were proceeding toward the "long-room," when Henderson called out from the loft:

"Who the devil air you, an' what ye want?"

"Better shet y'ur eyes an' years, 'Honest Jim,' so't you won't hev to lie when you tell the Vigilantes thet you don't know who tuck the pris'ner," returned Jack Fyffe, significantly.

"Ef you don't do nothin' else, why *I* won't know any on ye at all. An' ef ye like, jest take a good swig apiece, an' I'll charge it to profit an' loss," laughed the host, who apparently was not averse to having Poynter escape the doom that threatened him.

"Bully for you, ol' hoss; you won't lose any

thin' by it!" was the cry, and his invitation was complied with two or three times over.

Only pausing for one huge gulp of the liquor, Jack Fyffe unbarred the door, and soon severed the cords that hampered Poynter, who, after chafing his benumbed limbs, thanks to the skill Polk Redlaw had shown in drawing the knots, emerged from the long-room, a free man once more.

He glanced around him with not a little curiosity, scanning the forms and features of his rescuers as thoroughly as was practicable by the dim, flickering light cast by the one rude lamp. But if he recognized any of them, excepting Fyffe, he did not show it by word or sign.

"Come, boys," spoke up the tall man we have noted before, "we must make tracks, or those Vigilantes will be down upon us. They must have heard the rumpus, I reckon."

"But what shall we do with the prisoners—let them go?"

"No; take them along. We'll keep 'em as hostages, so that if any of our fellows are strung up, we can retaliate. Five of them, isn't there?"

"Yes; but about Sant?"

"Maltby?"

"Yes. He's dead."

"Take him along. If we leave him here, they'll toss him into the first hollow, and he was too good a man for that."

"You seem to be leader here, sir," said Poynter, placing a hand upon the man's shoulder. "What do you intend doing with me?"

"Well, that depends mainly upon yourself. If you have had enough of these Vigilance fellows, why, come with us. We never go back upon a fellow-craftsman," returned the man cordially.

"And you are—"

"The same as yourself; free livers is our name for it. Those whom we favor with our custom call us horse-thieves and counterfeiters," laughed the leader.

"Ah!" muttered Poynter, and bending his head as if in deep thought.

"All ready, Tamelt?"

"All ready, sir," was the prompt reply, and the little band left the house.

Jack Fyffe directed Poynter to a horse, which, with great delight and surprise, he found was his own noble bay, that had been taken when he was arrested. The five prisoners were also mounted, their horses having been found in the tavern stable; but they rode not by their own aid. Strong cords bound them to the saddle so securely that even had they tried to cast themselves to the ground, the effort would have been unsuccessful.

Poynter and Fyffe rode together, as they struck into a rapid lope along the soft, loamy road, but not until quite clear of the neighborhood, did either of them speak.

"Wal, we've sp'ilt the fun o' them hounds ter-morrer, 'tany rate," chuckled Fyffe.

"Yes, but how did it all come about?" queried Poynter, who did not appear very much at ease, when we consider what he had escaped.

"Wal, in co'se we wasn't a-goin' to see a fri'nd jerked up thet-a-way, 'thout helpin' 'im. So's soon as I see'd how it war gwine to work, I sent Sant Maltby to let the cap'n know, an' whar I'd meet 'em to 'xplain, like. Then we crawled up, an' tuck the guard, but poor Sant got throwed clean in his tracks. The rest you know."

"Who were the men you took prisoners?"

"Thar's one on 'em you'll be glad ter see—Jon'than Green."

"Ha!" exclaimed Poynter: "the lying scoundrel! But, Jack, my friend, do you know you've made a mistake?"

"How so?"

"I am no counterfeiter—never was."

"Thunder, you say!" ejaculated Fyffe.

"It's the truth," soberly affirmed Poynter. "I have never committed a deed against the law, to my knowledge, in my life."

"But the evidence?"

"Was one tissue of falsehood from first to last! Why it was started, or who was the one who planned it, I know no more than you do; but I will find out if it takes a lifetime," hotly exclaimed Poynter.

"Hello, my friends, what's up here?" asked the leader, falling back beside the two men, at the sound of Poynter's excited tones. "Not quarreling, I hope?"

"No, sir, I owe him too much for that," warmly responded Poynter. "But, are you the captain?"

"For the time being, I am. Why?" said the man, somewhat surprised at the other's tone.

"Then I must speak with you, for a moment."

"Go on; I have no secrets from Jack."

"Well," slowly uttered Poynter, "from what I have heard, I believe you labor under a serious mistake, regarding who and what I am."

"How so?" interrupted the leader. "Are not you the man that the Vigilance Committee arrested and condemned?"

"I am; as my back can testify!" bitterly gritted the young man.

"Well, then, where's the mistake?"

"In this: I was wrongfully accused. I have never, knowingly, passed a counterfeit coin, and as for murder, there is no blood upon my hands, save that shed in self-defense."

"Whe-ew!" whistled the outlaw. "But Jack told me the evidence was complete!"

"It was not his fault for thinking so. I would have believed the same in his place. But I am speaking the truth, and thought it best to tell you how the case stands, lest you should think me a traitor or a spy, in case the truth ever comes out."

"You were right. But what do you intend doing? The hunt will be hot for you, as, if a man would take all that trouble and expense to put you out of the way, legally, he will not let you off so easily."

"I know that; and in perfect freedom is the only chance of my ever clearing myself. I frankly own that I am puzzled," slowly replied Poynter.

"Well, sir, I am not often mistaken in a man, if I do say it myself," added the outlaw leader, after a pause. "And now I make you a proposition. Will you accept my hospitality for a few days, or weeks, until this excitement cools down?"

"Are you in earnest, and would you trust a stranger so far?" ejaculated Poynter, in astonishment.

"Not every one, I admit," laughed the other. "But you I can, and will; and if necessary, will answer to the band, for your honor, with my own life. But understand me: upon no account are you to divulge what you hear or see; nor the places we will take you to, even if your life depended upon it, unless we give you permission. And in return, you will be left free to come and go, as you will. You will not be asked, or expect'd, to do anything against your conscience; and if you should need any assistance that we can give, you have but to say as much."

"That is far more than I could expect, and I sincerely thank you for it," rejoined Poynter, warmly clasping the outlaw's hand. "But I am at a loss to imagine the cause of such generosity."

"It is easy told. You are an innocent man, unjustly accused and condemned; and I was once the same. False friends and misfortunes have made me what I now am, and I still have some of the better feeling in my heart, if I am an outcast, a branded felon.

"Besides, I feel a strange liking for you; why, or from what cause I know not, unless from the resemblance upon this one point."

"Well, sir," exclaimed the escaped prisoner, "I will gladly accept your offer, and if there is any return that I can make, without—"

"I understand you," interrupted the outlaw, with a tinge of melancholy in his tones, "and would be the last man in the world to ask you to forfeit your feeling of self-respect. But come," he added, again assuming his old air of reckless gayety. "We have fallen behind, and they'll think we are deserters. Spur up!"

"But one moment. Have we far to go?"

"Less than two miles, now," was the reply.

"But why?"

"Nothing much; only I would rather be in the neighborhood, for—"

"For certain reasons, I presume," laughed the outlaw leader. "But never mind, I was young once myself, although I don't look much like it now," and he ended with a half sigh.

Poynter's curiosity was keenly aroused by the language and manner of his strangely-acquired friend, so different from what might have been expected; and found himself wishing for a better chance to observe his features than was afforded by the dim, uncertain light.

As he peered toward him, Clay could see that it was a robust, powerful form, nearly if not quite as much so as his own. Of the features he could distinguish naught save the glitter of a pair of sparkling eyes, and the long, flowing hair of almost snowy whiteness, as was also the luxuriant beard and mustache.

As we said, Polk Redlaw resolved to dog the rescuing party wherever they might go, spurred on by his bitter hatred of Clay Poynter. And he was just the person to accomplish this if it lay in human power to do so.

When he saw Poynter emerge from the tavern under the bright glare of the torch carried by Jack Fyffe, unbound and in freedom, the heavy rifle rose as if by instinct to his cheek, and, for a moment, the wings of death again appeared to overshadow the young man.

But the gun was lowered. The mongrel was not satisfied with such a revenge. His hatred was too intense; he required a death of shame— of degradation; a death that would destroy both the life and honor of his foe, and leave a record at which the finger of scorn and contempt would be pointed.

When the cavalcade plunged into the darkness of the tree-shadowed road, the human bloodhound followed hard upon the scent. His rifle trailed in one hand, his head and neck craned forward, Polk Redlaw sped along with noiseless strides that appeared to be made without an effort.

So steady, silent and uniform was his progress that it seemed like a magnificent piece of machinery, rather than a man. His Indian blood shone forth now in his free and untrammeled motion, as he kept at a certain distance in the rear of the rescuers, the same whether they rode fast or slow.

From his crouching position he could not be seen upon the shadowed road, while those whom he was trailing, being mounted, could quite plainly be distinguished. But for a time we must turn elsewhere.

CHAPTER VII.

A SAD HISTORY.

WHEN Neil McGuire returned home from the "Twin Sycamores," disgusted at the brutality displayed by his neighbors and comrades, he found his daughter Nora sitting up awaiting him, late as it was, the fearful suspense and terror she had endured plainly imprinted upon her pale and worn countenance.

Shocked at the change, and strongly excited by the events of the last few hours, McGuire told her all, winding up by saying that he feared the prisoner would not live to see another day dawn. Nora gave one low cry and swooned, and when she recovered from it a strong fever set in.

There was no doctor nearer than the fort, even if he could be induced to journey so far, and as old Aunt Eunice had gained quite a reputation as a nurse, she was called in, while the almost distracted father set out for medical aid. The doctor came, but his aid was not needed; the fever had been broken, and, strange to say, Nora was up and about the house in as apparent good health as ever.

But if the worthy farmer was surprised, we, who are in the secret, need not be. It was, perhaps, owing to a certain message brought by Aunt Eunice, who kindly turned her back while it was being perused, and when she did look it had disappeared; but from the frequent journeys made by the invalid's hand to the region of the heart, it is not difficult to guess where.

The note was from Clay Poynter, briefly detailing the facts of his escape, stating that he was in a place of safety, and imploring an interview, leaving the time and place to her, of which he could be informed by Aunt Eunice. Nora did not hesitate about granting the request, but the return of her father necessitated a postponement, greatly to the disappointment of the lover, who was disgusted at only meeting his old housekeeper when he expected a sweetheart.

Neil McGuire was sorely puzzled and disturbed about something, and soon opened his mind to Nora the day of his return. It was after supper, and she had brought him his filled pipe, when he bade her sit down—that he had something to tell her.

"Do you know, pet, that I half-way fear we have been doing Clay Poynter a great injustice?"

"Oh, father, I knew it all along!"

"Did you, indeed? Well, as I said, I am afraid we have been mistaken, although I am not quite certain. And the reason I think so is this:

"It was late in the evening when I got to the fort, and as the doctor would not start out that same night, I went over to the city; as I could not bear to sit still while thinking of the danger you might be in. It was raining, and feeling cold and chilly, I stepped into a saloon to get a drink, when I met a man who was just a-coming out.

"I was so astonished that you could have knocked me down with a wheat-straw, for I would have sworn he was none other than *John Dement!* But while I stood there, he slipped out, and when I started after him, he was gone. I hunted for an hour, but without success; I could not find him again."

"And there was no mistake?" anxiously asked Nora.

"There *may* have been. I might have been deceived, and took some other person for him. If it *was* Dement, he had his whiskers colored black, and his hair trimmed, and of the same color. But I caught his full eye, and you know it is not a common one."

"Yes, it makes me think of a rattlesnake's," shuddered the maiden.

"Well, even if he is innocent about the murder, there is the other charge," added McGuire.

"But that may be false, too."

"I don't think so. And yet," he added, after a slight pause, "he didn't act like a guilty man."

Nora did not answer, although strongly tempted to do so, for fear she would reveal more than was prudent, and in a short time both retired.

A little after noon, on the next day, had Neil McGuire glanced up from his work back of the house and looked almost due west, he would have seen the trim, dainty form of his daughter, as she disappeared in the woods, accompanied by Aunt Eunice. And perhaps his mind would have been still more perturbed had he witnessed the fervor with which a certain stalwart, handsome man embraced Nora, while her antiquated duenna placidly stared at the bushy top of a neighboring tree.

Whatever it was Aunt Eunice saw, it must have been *very* interesting, for there she stared, and never once looked around until her name was called. Then she seated herself at a little distance from the lovers, pulling out from her pocket a huge stocking, that could only be intended for one person in the settlement, unless worn upon both feet at once, industriously knitting, as deaf now as she had been blind before.

We need record but one passage in the conversation, as the remainder was foreign to our purpose.

"Well, pet, I will explain what your father meant when alluding to my leaving Kentucky. It is true, I did leave there to save my life, much as I fled from here, although matters had not gone quite so far then.

"When I was but a child, my father was accused—falsely, as I ever will maintain, although I have no proof—of belonging to Sturdevant's gang of counterfeiters and horse-thieves. He was arrested and thrown into prison, but he never had a trial. A band of disguised men forced the jail, and taking him from his cell, proceeded to a grove some four miles distant, and hung him like a dog!

"It was nearly a month before the remains were found, by a man hunting cattle, and then, after his burial, my mother sickened, dying within the same year. I was but eleven years old then, and although so young, these fearful events made me desperate.

"The neighbors all looked upon me as a sort of outcast, and taught their children to shun me as though I were a moral pest. This did not help me much, and as I grew older, I was taunted and hooted at, for my father's *crime!*

"But, as my muscles grew they found this fast becoming a dangerous sport, for I bitterly resented every insult, even from those twice and thrice my own age. I had no relations, not even a friend to lean upon, or to whom I could turn for aid or counsel. And thus I grew up!

"I admit being wild and reckless; but I can honestly say that I never once committed a mean or criminal deed. And yet I was often accused in whispers, of being both a counterfeiter and a horse-thief! Almost any one would have left the place in disgust; but I did not. The only beings that I had ever loved were lying in the little yard back of our house.

"I often, when my trials had been unusually bitter, have spent the livelong night beside the graves of my parents, sobbing as if my heart would break; and it is to those sacred influences alone that I attribute my remaining clear of a life of crime.

"Well, I was at length openly arrested, but as I managed to escape before trial, I never learned who was my accuser. It would have been almost certain death to remain there then, as I had no friends who could assist me to clear myself, and so I fled.

"I went to Arkansas, near Merton, and for a time all went well. I entered a homestead, and for several years I worked diligently on it; and then sold it for a fair price, intending to open a store. But my enemies followed me even there, and the same suspicions were noised about. I was avoided by all respectable persons as though I had the plague.

"In disgust I left the place, and from that time until I came here, I wandered far and near, living an aimless life until I thought I had once more eluded my pursuers. But you have seen how sadly I was mistaken; and here, just as life was brightest, the same rumors were whispered abroad, the old charges were brought up against me. I was seized and flogged like a dog!"

"Poor Clay!" murmured Nora, through the ⸺ called forth by the sad history of her lover's life, as she clasped his hand in hers, as if to still further testify her boundless faith in his truth and honesty.

"Yes, but I go no further. I have found *you*, and now I have an additional incentive to clear myself, and baffle my secret enemy, whoever he may be. But how?—that is the question."

After some further conversation, and an appointment being made for another meeting, the lovers separated, Nora and Eunice returning to the house, while Poynter walked rapidly away toward his own building.

CHAPTER VIII.
A DELECTABLE CONFAB.

AFTER leaving Nora, Poynter walked swiftly in the direction of his own house, that had been closed ever since Aunt Eunice had been called in to attend Nora during her sickness. But he kept a good lookout as he proceeded, lest he should be discovered by some of those kind friends whose hospitality he had abandoned so hastily, a few days before.

He had found a secure refuge with the outlaw band who had rescued him from the power of the Vigilance Committee, where he resolved to remain until his plans for the future were fully matured, at the urgent request of the leader. This man had evinced a strong interest in Poynter, and pledged his own as well as the assistance of the band, if it should prove necessary, in any way.

Just as Poynter was about to cross the crest of a hill, he heard the quick thud of a horse's hoofs coming at full speed upon the opposite side of the rise, and darted at once into the thicket of bushes upon the left side of the road. Cautiously parting the leafy screen, so that he could observe the extreme summit of the rise, Poynter awaited the horseman's approach.

Scarcely had he done so when the rider rose the crest, and drawing rein, paused and glanced around him. With a half-surprised curse, Poynter raised his heavy rifle, while the sharp click sounded clear and distinct as the hammer was sprung back; but then he lowered it.

"The lying dog! For a cent I'd plug him, if only to save 'Judge Lynch' a job."

The horse and rider were standing out in bold relief against the clear sky, but still the ambushed fugitive could tell that Polk Redlaw, the half-breed, stood before him.

Redlaw appeared to be expecting some one, as Clay judged from his manner, and after a few minutes' waiting, he placed his fingers to his mouth, and blew a shrill, piercing blast, that echoed from point to point before dying down to nothing. Scarcely had the sounds ceased, when a second peal came whistling along the ridge, as if in answer; to which Polk replied, and then dismounted.

In a few moments a second man appeared upon foot, with his long rifle carried at a trail, and the two men greeted each other as if greatly pleased at the meeting. Again the steely glitter shone in Poynter's eyes, while he bit his lips fiercely as if to repress his emotions, when he recognized the new-comer.

"Ah!" he gritted, as he crouched forward. "Wesley Sprowl! There's deviltry on foot wh such men meet together, and by all that's good, I'll scent it out!"

The two men now plunged into a little side-trail, Redlaw leading his horse, and no sooner had they disappeared than Poynter retreated until around the bend, where he glided across the road, and in a few moments struck their trail; keeping just without the path, where, by any chance the men he was dogging should glance back, he would be out of sight.

They proceeded leisurely enough, and he had no difficulty in keeping within ear-shot of the horse's tread, while his own footsteps were deadened upon the moist soil. After proceeding thus for nearly half a mile, the two men paused, and slipping the bit from his horse's mouth, Polk Redlaw allowed it to feed at will while he and Sprowl seated themselves upon the greensward beneath a huge oak tree.

Poynter, by dint of cautious creeping, managed to gain a dense clump of bushes at only a few yards in the rear of their position, where he crouched down with his weapons ready for instant use, in case he should be discovered. But they gave no sign of suspecting an intruder, and conversed in an easy, careless style, very much to Poynter's edification. The first of this he missed, owing to the task he had to perform, but he listened intently.

"Well," Polk Redlaw was saying, "they did not suspect any person was following them, although I kept them in sight the entire distance. And that was no slouch of a job either, for they were in a lope most of the way, and I began to be pretty well blown before they gave any signs of halting.

"But then they paused and a signal was sounded; and from the reply I knew that I had dogged them home. And I was right, for in another ten minutes the whole crowd was gathered in a huddle, unsaddling their horses, while a dozen or so more were building fires as if the entire country belonged to them.

"I lay low, taking notes, and I saw enough in the next hour to satisfy me that I had really tracked them to the den of the horse-thieves; for there were several tents and regular fireplaces fixed up, while the ground was tramped hard and dry."

"And where was that?" inquired Sprowl, curiously.

"Well, you'll let it go no further, of course," added Redlaw, after a slight pause. "You know where Han Hooker killed the big bear, last fall; near the 'Turkey branch?' Just due West along the creek about a quarter, is the spot.

"But as I was spying around, a cursed dog somehow got scent of me, and as I saw him circling around, I lit out, for if they had found me there, nothing would have saved my hide. I cut sticks in a hurry, as I got out of their hearing, but the brute took my trail, and in a few moments I could hear him coming, hot foot, growling like a painter.

"I was afraid to burn powder, so I just hunkered down behind a big rock, and drew my butcher. As the imp turned the corner, I grabbed his nose and twisted him down; then a cut or two and *he* was quieted.

"But I'd seen enough, so I started for home,

with the dog on my shoulder—for I was afraid to leave him where the knife-cuts might 'a' told tales—and carried him until at a safe distance, when I dropped him over the bank into the creek. And there my infernal luck still followed me, for his claw caught in my shirt and over I went, head-first, plump onto the rocks.

"Luckily my head took the dog for a pillow, and only got a little bruised and stunned-like; but when I came to I found that my right ankle was either broken or badly sprained. I managed to climb up to the level, although every motion nearly made me yell out, but there I was stuck!

"I knew that if my life depended upon it, I could not have got to the town, as I was, and so I lay there, thinking what to do next. At last I slid down the bank, cut off a hind quarter of the dog, and then managed to drag myself to the 'Hole-in-the-Wall'—you remember?—where I lay until this morning two hours after sunrise, I saw a horse—that one yonder, it was—straying along the branch, and as he was tame I managed to catch him; rigged a halter from a piece of lime-bark, and lit out for town, where I got, safe and sound, after giving you the hint to meet me here."

"Well, what'd you want, anyhow?" asked Sprowl.

"In a moment. You see I told old Reeves about the hole I'd found, and offered to guide him to it, after dark, to-night. So he sent out messengers, and by this time the Vigilantes are all up to snuff.

"You may be called on to help, but if so, I want you to play sick; have a thundering shake, or something of the sort."

"Just what I'd 'a' done anyhow," dryly responded Sprowl. "I have no notion of running my head into the hands of that cursed Poynter. Meagreson didn't pay me for *that*."

"Well then, you'd just as lieve make a 'double sawbuck' as not, if by doing so you spite Poynter and run no risks?"

"Twenty dollars?"

"Yes. And for half an hour's work."

"Wouldn't I? Why the old man only gave me a hundred for swearing against Poynter—Hello! what's that?" he added, starting to his feet, and looking toward the bushes where Poynter was concealed.

The latter had given a sudden start, as he caught the hint dropped by Sprowl, that could only refer to the charge of murder that had been brought against him. But who was this Meagreson, or the "old man?"

"Bah!" grunted Polk, lazily turning his head, "don't get scart at your own shadow. I heard it too, but it's only my horse. Come. I'm in a hurry. Will you earn the money?"

"That depends," replied the other as he re-seated himself, "upon what it is."

"Well, I know you'll never peach—"

"Of course not!"

"I know it," dryly added Redlaw; "it wouldn't be healthy. But I want you to be sick when the crowd starts to-night, and then after about two hours—say about midnight—you must get up and set the house yonder on fire."

"What!"

"Set the house of Clay Poynter on fire—isn't that plain enough? Never you mind what for—that's my own affair. It's enough that I've good reasons, and when I come back, I'll tell you. Will you do it?"

"It's a risky job—" hesitated Sprowl.

"No it isn't, either. But, yes or no, because if you won't, there's others—"

"Enough! I'll do it. But cash down, you know," leered Sprowl.

"Well, there's half of it. The rest I'll hand you in the morning."

"But supposing you should get rubbed out to-night?" suggested Sprowl.

"Curse your croaking!" hotly exclaimed Redlaw, thrusting out another bill. "There; will that do?"

"Yes; but say, isn't it a good joke upon old Meagreson that he has been paying us all to prove this Poynter a counterfeiter and murderer, while all the time he really belonged to the gang?" chuckled Sprowl.

"Bet ye! But come now, old fellow," added Redlaw, insinuatingly, "who is the old coon, anyhow? I know you can tell a fellow, if you will."

"Maybe I will, when you tell me what for you want the house fired," significantly answered Sprowl.

"Well, give me an idee, anyhow," urged Polk. "I'll tell you to-morrow, sure."

"Honest?"

"I said so, didn't I?" sharply.

"Well, don't get your back up about it and I will give you a hint, anyhow. You see, I knew him in Kentucky, and again in Illinois, where he helped run the business, after Sturdevant—"

"What!"

"Fact. I done a little in that line myself, on the sly, and we were thrown together consid'rable, as he furnished the 'queer.' But I got the pull on him in a little scrape in which a certain named Duaber was concerned.

"There was a love-affair mixed up with it, I believe, and while Meagreson got the sack, Duaber got the girl. So a lot of charges were trumped up, much as we've served this Poynter, you know, only it ended in the poor devil's being lynched in earnest.

"He was taken from jail and hung by a gang spurred on by the old man, although he was not present at the deed. I gained a cool thousand in square money for it, and all went off smoothly. But I thought he was dead until he came here, found me out, gave me some money, and got me to play the same trick over again."

"I wonder what his reasons were anyhow," mused Polk. "I'd give a five-spot to know," he added, covertly glancing at Sprowl.

"You will?"

"If it's honest, I wouldn't mind."

"I know what you're up to," nodded the other, "but if you'll promise me not to breathe a word or hint of who told you, to *anybody*, I'll tell you?"

"You know—or should know by this time, that I never split on a friend."

"That's so, Polk, and if you'll shell out, I'll tell you in a cat's whisper."

"Here you are; but no shenanigan, now," replied Polk, handing the bill to his comrade.

"Honor bright! Well, then, this Clay Poynter, as he calls himself, is in reality none other than Henry Duaber the son of James Duaber, who was hung on a false charge by the Vigilance Committee!"

"Whew!" echoed Polk Redlaw, with a long-drawn breath of astonishment. "I begin to see into it now. And the old man hates the son for the father's sake!"

"Yes, that's just it. And as you've acted on the square, so far, I don't mind telling that he is the same one who has hunted this young fellow from pillar to post, ever since he was a little shaver," said Sprowl, confidentially.

"I'd rather have his friendship than his hatred, then," laughed Polk. "When's he coming back, do you know?"

"Not yet awhile. It'd spoil the whole thing, you see; if 'John Dement' should come to life again before Poynter was nailed."

"But it seems to me that you'll be in a bad box, my friend, if it is found out that you swore to a lie."

"Oh, that's easy patched up. Besides, the men will be so cut up and ashamed at being greened so, that they'll be glad enough to let the matter drop, and as for the *law*, I'd die of old age before that could or would do anything here." sneered Sprowl.

"Well, that's your lookout, not mine. But we'd better be moving. Catch my horse for me, won't you?—this cursed ankle is sore yet."

In a few moments the mongrel was mounted, and paused to add:

"Now mind you play your part. And not before eleven, anyhow, as if the glow should be seen too soon, the men will turn back, thinking it some of theirs."

"All right. But you send around for me; it'll look better. I'll go home now and begin shaking," and with a loud laugh the two precious scoundrels separated.

Scarcely had they disappeared when Clay Poynter emerged from his ambush, and stood for a moment trembling with anger.

Truly, he had good cause for being wrathy, and for feeling thoughtful, too, in the revelations so complacently made by Wesley Sprowl.

But he did not pause long; then throwing his rifle across his shoulder, he struck through the woods at a rapid pace, heading his course toward the rendezvous of "White Crees," the leader of the band who had rescued him from the "Twin Sycamores."

CHAPTER IX.
THE INCENDIARY.

IT was some time after dark before Clay Poynter neared the rendezvous of the border outlaws, despite the speed at which he traveled. But he was in time, and after satisfying the sentinel of his identity, he hastened at once to the presence of "White Crees," as his aged friend was universally termed by his men and comrades.

He was lying at full length upon the ground, one elbow propping his head as he gazed thoughtfully into the fire, crackling merrily before him. There was a kind of half-frown upon his face and a fiery gleam in his full black eyes, that told Poynter he was unusually excited about something.

"Well, sir, what is it?" quickly asked Crees, as he raised his head at the young man's approach.

"Bad news, I fear. This retreat is known—"
"The deuce!"
"Yes; and you will be attacked to-night by the Vigilance Committee, in full force," coolly rejoined Poynter.

"Bad enough, I must say. But are you certain?"

"If hearing the entire plan, detailed by the man that found you out, is enough, I am."

"So—so!" muttered the outlaw chief.

"Well, your decision," impatiently said Clay, "what is it?"

"We must run for it. Not but that we are strong enough to stand our ground, if such a course would be prudent, but we must tread lightly. The country is hot enough now, and a collision, where blood would be shed, must be avoided."

"Very well, then; I want one man for duty concerning myself, as a sort of witness. Can I have him?"

"A dozen, if you say so," was the cordial reply. "Who is he?"
"Jack Fyffe."
"Hyar I be, square, an' mighty glad ef I kin help ye any."

"Then saddle our horses as quick as possible, please. If I had time," again turning to the outlaw leader, "I would explain, as I have much to tell; but some other time must do. Things are working around a little, and I may come out right side up after all."

"Good! and I, too, have done a good job to-day."

"So? Where'll we find you?"

"Tell Jack to lead you to the north side of 'Bald Hill,' where the branch cuts through the 'Wildcat Range.' He knows it well."

"Well, I must be off, and the sooner *you* are, the better. It's nearly ten o'clock now, and they'll be along by one at the latest."

"So they may," laughed the outlaw, "but thanks to your warning, they'll find little to satisfy their appetite. Remember, 'Bald Hill.'"

"All right!" and then the young man vaulted into the saddle as Fyffe led up the horses, and the two men dashed rapidly along the road.

"Now Jack, old fellow," cried Poynter, "we must ride as if the 'gentleman in black' was at our horses' tails, or we'll be too late."

"Whar to?"

"My house. Do you know a path that we can go, so as to avoid meeting our friends, who'll take the main road?"

"Bet ye! It's rough ridin', though, but bein's it's shorter, 'twon't take no longer. What's the biz?"

Thereupon Poynter succinctly stated what he had heard while eavesdropping the two precious scoundrels, adding:

"It isn't that I care so much for the house, but we must take that Sprowl a prisoner. He knows enough to clear me, and if he can prove what he said, to bring this Dement or Meagreson to justice; and that's just my hand now."

"We'll do it. Ef not in the act, we'll nab him at his own shanty. Meagreson, ye said?"

"Yes; do you know him?"

"Oh, no, I guess not! Lord, won't the ol' man be glad!"

"Crees, do you mean?"

"Look out! Hyar's the 'cut-off. Foller me cluss an' look out for your head."

They now diverged from the road into a path just allowing one horse to pass at a time, and the riders were forced to stoop low along their horses' necks to keep from being struck by the low-hanging limbs.

Presently the ground grew more open, although they still continued in single file, and as they rose the crest of a hill, Fyffe exclaimed, in a glad tone:

"It's all hunky so fur anyhow, square. Ef it stays so fur ten minutes longer, we'll save 'em both."

"Are we so near, then?"

"Leetle better'n a mile. See, thar's the branch."

"Good! I know where we are now. Spur along; we've no time to lose."

In less than the time named the horsemen drew rein at the western fence of the yard, and speedily hitching the animals, they stealthily advanced until the rear of the house was gained. After pausing for a moment to listen, and hearing nothing suspicious, they made the circuit of the building; thus satisfying themselves that the would-be incendiary had not yet arrived.

"We're in good time, Jack," whispered Poynter, joyfully, "and 'll get him yet. Do you hide here in front, and I'll do the same behind. If you need help, whistle and I'll come."

"Help, ag'in' thet little or'nary cuss? Bah! I'd take him 'ith one finger. Shall I nab 'im as soon as I see him?"

"No; I guess we'd better let him start a blaze first. Then he can't deny but what that was his intention. Yes, that's the best way."

"All right, then. Better lumber down, though, fer ef he shed cotch a glimpse o' either on us, it's all played," cautioned Fyffe.

This advice was too good not to be followed, and in a moment more, all was still and silent about the premises. Poynter's mind was greatly excited, as well it might be, at the facts he had learned on that day; and as the gloomy prospect that had spread over his future began to lighten a thousand air-castles were built, over all of which the pleasing form of Nora McGuire, his little rosy Irish lass, reigned as queen.

But he was suddenly aroused from his reverie by the light tramp of a man's feet, and glancing up, he saw a dim, shadowy figure cautiously approaching the house, at a little to his left. From his position close beside the slightly elevated porch that stood in the rear of the kitchen, the door of which led out upon it, Poynter was perfectly hidden, while yet he could quite plainly note the intruder's every movement.

This person lightly stepped upon the porch and cautiously tried the door, but it was fastened. Then he went to one of the rear windows, and after a slight effort, raised it; then propping it up with a stick, drew himself through the aperture.

Listening intently, Poynter heard him groping around the room, and then, after a few moments' silence, he saw a faint, flickering light spring up. Gliding to the window, he peered through, and saw Wesley Sprowl igniting a short piece of tallow-dip by the aid of a match.

Poynter knew now that he had his game secure, and crept around the building, where he was met by Jack Fyffe, who had been alarmed by the slight noise, and was just coming around to investigate it.

"Is it him?"

"Yes," whispered Poynter, "but we must let him start the fire first, before we interrupt him. Then as I jump through the window, do you burst in the back door and put out the blaze. I'll 'tend to him."

"Jest as you say, square; on'y I'd like to gi'n the varmint a squoze, like, jest fer beans," grunted Fyffe, as he followed Poynter around the building.

They could still see the light, and hear an increased rattling in the room, and cautiously peering in at one corner of the window, the two men saw the incendiary splitting fine kindlings with the knife he had drawn from his belt. Poynter could scarcely restrain his passion, at noting how coolly and deliberately the dastardly scoundrel set about his work.

When a little pile of the shavings were made Sprowl piled over them some splinters of wood that lay beside the kitchen stove, and then applied the lighted candle to the heap. It instantly ignited, the tiny blaze creeping along, thrusting out its forked tongue like a serpent; at which the incendiary gave a chuckle of delight, and rising, dropped a chair over the fire.

He next grasped the table, with the same intention, but Poynter had seen enough, and drawing himself up by the arms, he dropped lightly through the window—the noise made by Sprowl in dragging the table effectually drowning his footsteps. One stride, and the large, muscular right hand of Clay Poynter tightly clasped the villain by the neck, compressing it as if in a vise.

Jack Fyffe was in nowise behindhand, but speedily followed his leader through the open window, thinking that better than to demolish the door, especially as there was no particularly urgent call for haste; and with a few shoves of his huge foot, kicked the brands into the capacious fireplace, it having done no damage, save slightly scorching the chairs and floor.

"It may be fun to you, square, da'say 'tis, but ef you 'xpects to git any 'fessions outen thet critter, you'd do well to let up a little," admonished Jack, as he bent forward to peer into the face of the prisoner.

And there was ample foundation for his warning, for in his rage at the cowardly miscreant's action, Poynter threw the whole power of his arm into the grasp, and Sprowl was already senseless.

"You're right, Jack," said Poynter, as he relaxed his grip and suffered Sprowl to drop upon the floor, then bending over him, he poured a little brandy down his throat.

In a few moments Sprowl had recovered sufficiently to sit up, thoroughly bewildered at the sudden reverse he had experienced. But his captors did not give him time to ponder over it, or ask questions, as it was growing late, and for obvious reasons they did not care to remain longer than was absolutely necessary in the neighborhood.

So, after securely binding the incendiary's hands behind his back, the two men, highly elated at their complete success, led the way to where the horses were hitched.

"You're the lightest, Jack," said Poynter; "better take him up behind you on the horse."

"Durn the thief!" growled Fyffe, "let 'im tramp it; 't'll do him good."

"So he might; but there's no telling whom we may meet, and I won't lose him now. But if you object, he can ride with me."

"I didn't think o' that, square. Jest you hyste him up arter I mount."

This was speedily done, and Sprowl secured to the body of his captor, thus effectually preventing all hopes of an escape. Then leaving the premises they entered the road, proceeding at a moderate pace, as they were not desirous of arousing any of the neighbors who might chance to be at home.

For a couple of hours they rode on without halting, when they both drew rein simultaneously, bending forward in the saddles, and listening eagerly. It was a sharp, clear report, followed by what appeared an irregular volley of small-arms, resounding all about them as if an entire army was engaged in battle.

But the two men were far too well versed in the peculiarities of that portion of the country not to know that it was but the multiplied reverberations of the one first shot.

"Listen!" exclaimed Poynter, guardedly, "don't you hear the click of shoes upon the stones?"

"Y'ur right, by the 'tarnal! It's the Vigilantys, I reckon. Better kiver."

"To the left," muttered Poynter, leading the way. "Hold the reins while I keep the horses from neighing. And mark you, Sprowl, those are your friends, but if you utter so much as a whisper, by the God above me, I will shoot you like a dog! You know I keep my word. They may hunt us, but it would be too late to do *you* any good!" hissed the young man as he passed by the prisoner.

They were scarcely a dozen feet from the road, upon a little lower ground, from whence they could have a clear view of anybody passing by. There was no moon, and the dense growth of underbrush close behind them, added to the dark color of their horses, rendered discovery very improbable, if not impossible.

Poynter stood by the animals' heads, one hand upon the muzzle of each, to check any inclination they might feel for whickering during the passage of the horsemen. They had not long to wait.

Scarcely had these precautions been taken, when the foremost man came in sight, and then the main body. Their oaths and curses, if nothing else, would have identified them as the band of Vigilantes, returning from an unsuccessful search for the outlaws, thanks to Poynter's timely warning.

After waiting a few minutes, until satisfied that the entire band had passed, the ambushed men again entered the road, proceeding for some little distance in silence. Then Clay spoke:

"Those fellows weren't in the best of humor, eh, Jack?"

"Not overly much. Wal, it shows 'at the boys got cl'ar, anyhow. But see, hyar's the cut-off."

"Leading to Bald Hill?"

"Yas," and Fyffe led the way along a narrow, irregular path.

CHAPTER X.

SPROWL TOES THE MARK.

IN less than half an hour the tall, rocky crest of "Bald Hill" reared its gray head before the men, and Poynter gave vent to a sigh of relief as he saw that the tiresome ride was nearly at an end.

The outlaws were upon the alert, as the quick, sharp challenge testified when the outer lines were reached. Dismounting with a half-groan, Poynter relieved Fyffe of his "back-load," and after securely binding the man, dropped him upon the ground, asking the sentry to keep an eye upon him. Then Poynter threw himself beneath a tree, and almost ere his limbs were still, a fast-increasing rumbling, as of very distant thunder, told how sound was his slumber.

The sun was an hour above the horizon when Poynter again opened his eyes, although he declared he hadn't five winks of sleep. But after a cool bath at the creek, close at hand, he felt greatly refreshed, and joined White Crees, who was sitting near one of the fires, smoking a pipe.

"Up for all day, Poynter?"

"Well, I hardly know, to tell the truth," laughed Clay. "I can tell you better after I have some grub."

"There's part of a cold turkey, or here's venison; take your choice."

"Hot meat for me, even if I do have to turn cook to get it," said Poynter, cutting several generous slices from the prime saddle that hung suspended from a tree near at hand. "But, hello, I forgot! What has been done with my prisoner that I brought in last night, or, rather, this morning?"

"I put him in a safe place," returned the outlaw. "The poor devil was nearly dead this morning. You put him with his head downhill, and I really believe that another hour would have finished him."

"'Twouldn't be a very great pity," muttered Poynter, his mouth full of meat, "after I have got out of him what I want to know. And that makes me think—where's Jack?"

"Off on a hunt, I believe; a gang of turkeys passed down the creek this morning, and he's after them. But why?"

"Nothing; only from a hint that he dropped last night about one Meagreson—"

"What! *Meagreson*, did you say?" excitedly exclaimed the outlaw, bending forward, clutching Poynter with his long, bony fingers by the arm, until the young man winced with pain.

"Thunder! yes, but I ain't made of wood, nor steel either. Do you want to take off my arm?"

"Pardon, Poynter; but that name made me forget myself. Where did *you* hear of *him?*"

"From Sprowl; he told Polk Redlaw a long yarn yesterday that I overheard, and enough in it to show me that my secret foe was this Meagreson, or John Dement, as he called himself here."

"Tell me all, just as he said it, I have good

reasons for wanting to hear it," added the outlaw, impressively.

Poynter gave a hasty outline, and to his great surprise Crees bowed his head to the earth, his strong form working and writhing as if in mortal agony. But when he would have stopped, a hoarsely-whispered "*Go on*" from the old man was his only answer.

"And now you know as much as I do," added Clay, arising. "But come, show me where you put Sprowl, and I will see if he can tell me anything more."

Crees arose without a word, and passed a short distance up the hillside, pressing through some bushes until he stood at the foot of a good-sized tree, in a tiny glade. To the trunk of this, and in an upright position, was bound the form of the wretched Sprowl.

Poynter started back in half-alarm at the fearful change a few hours had made in the man's appearance. Dreadfully haggard and sickly-looking, with his eyes protruding, his tongue lolling from his parched jaws, the drops of cold sweat rolling over his face, Sprowl looked as if about to give up the ghost in earnest.

"My God! he's dying," cried Poynter, as he sprung forward and severed the cords that bound the poor devil, laying him down upon the ground.

"Give me your flask; mine's empty," as he turned to Crees, who silently handed it to him, while his eyes were fixed intently upon the wretch's face.

A few swallows were poured down Sprowl's throat, and thus bathing his face and neck with the pungent liquor, Poynter soon uttered a glad cry. In truth, the patient appeared to be recovering, and in a few minutes the light of reason once more shone in his eyes.

"I know that man," slowly ejaculated Crees, not once removing his gaze, that appeared to attract the other's attention much the same as the fascination exercised by the rattlesnake.

"My God! who are you?" almost yelled the wretch, as he suddenly sat up, staring at Crees, wildly.

"Who should know better than you, Wesley Sprowl?" sternly said the outlaw.

"I know you now. You are—"

"Hold!" commanded Crees, "that name is dead now. If you as much as whisper it before I tell you, by all that's holy, I'll treat you as I would a snake! Do you understand?"

"Yes, sir," faltered Sprowl, once more sinking back.

"Here," interrupted Poynter, checking this by-play, that not a little excited his curiosity. "Here, Sprowl, take another sup of brandy. I want you to answer me some questions, and you'll need your strength before we're through."

"Yes—yes—the brandy!" eagerly muttered the prisoner, clutching at the bottle, and not drawing breath until it was emptied. "There! now I can talk; only I am hungry," he added, wistfully.

"Well, I will get you something, for I am going to treat you a deuced sight better than you deserve, after your lies about me."

"They *were* lies, all of them; but I will confess—yes, I will confess!"

"Just stick to that, old fellow, and my word for it, you'll never have cause to repent doing so," cheerily replied Poynter. "Now, Mr. Crees, if you'll just stay here to keep our friend company, like, I'll go get something for him to eat."

"Gladly; for I, too, have something to ask Mr. Sprowl," returned the outlaw. "And, if you will, please give a whistle when you come back; won't you?"

"Certainly, if you wish it."

"I do. But don't be offended," he added appealingly. "I will explain it all to you soon. And anything else that may appear strange, that you wish to know. Will that do?"

"Finely," cordially replied Poynter, pressing his strange friend's hand, and then dashing down the hillside to the encampment fires.

He cut some venison steaks, and soon had them broiling merrily, after which he prepared hot water for coffee, and stirred up a "hoe-cake," standing it upon a strip of elm-bark to bake before the glowing embers.

When his cookery was completed, Poynter gave the desired signal, and when he reached the tree found that the outlaw was sitting in the same spot, while Sprowl had bowed his head between his hands, evidently deeply moved by some emotion, either of fear or remorse. But the young man quelled the curiosity he felt, for he knew that Crees's word might be trusted, and that ere long all would be explained.

"Well, old fellow, here you are," cheerily cried Poynter, as he placed the food and drink before Sprowl, with not a trace of rancor in his tones. "And do you see how fast you can demolish them, while I do a little talking. But mind you, don't answer before you've weighed well what you say, as you may have to swear to it. Do you hear?"

"Yes, sir, I do hear, and so help me God, I'll tell the honest truth if it hangs me!" solemnly exclaimed the prisoner. "You treat me and talk to me like a gentleman, while I have treated you and yours worse than a dog. I shall say nothing but the truth, and if it must be, will swear it before any court."

"Now I begin to know you again," cried Clay, gladly; "and I tell you that, guilty as you have been, unless you have helped commit one deed—"

"Your father, you mean?" interrupted Sprowl.

"Yes."

"As God hears me, I never raised a finger against his life. I falsely swore against his honor, I do not deny, but of anything further, I am innocent."

"Well, go on and eat. I'll tell you my terms, although I frankly tell you that were it not for your wife and helpless family, I would *demand* not *request*. Now, however, we will let that pass.

"First, I wish you to tell me the plot against my father; who concocted it, and who were the prominent actors in it. Also their reasons for so doing, so far as you are aware of them.

"Then what you know of myself; who it was that has hunted me from 'pillar to post,' to use your own language. Also what you know about one Meagreson, *alias* John Dement, his character, crimes, and, in short, everything.

"I warn you, however, that I am not to be deceived; that I know far more than you have any idea of, so that any attempt of that kind will only injure yourself. Do you fully comprehend me?" queried Poynter.

Sprowl answered by a double nod; his mouth being crammed so full of the juicy deer-steak, that speech was impossible.

"Very well. Now, I will tell you further. If you make a clean breast of it, however guilty you may have been, with that one exception, I will let you go free, and in addition give you such a start that, if you endeavor to do so, you can live an honest, comfortable life.

"I will pay for your farm, I will build you a house and stock them both, so that you can have no further excuse for going to the bad. But mark me—this is not on *your* account; it is for your patient, long-suffering wife, and the deeds will be given in her name. Now, what do you say to the bargain?"

"Well, sir, what *can* I say," muttered Sprowl, brokenly, " but that while I have acted like a dog, you treat me like a white man? Perhaps 'twould be a better job if you put me beyond the way of doing any more harm; I *do* think so. I have always been a cursed, cowardly fool, and if at times I would try—and God knows that I *have* tried for Mary's sake and the children's—to break off, here would come a temptation, and down I'd go, worse than ever," gloomily replied the prisoner.

"Well," heartily responded Poynter, "better times are coming now, and if you will only help yourself, others will lend a hand. Cheer up, old fellow, and hold your head up like an honest man; there's a heap of good left in you yet, or you'd never talk as you do now."

"If I ever *do* get on my feet again, it is to you and *him* that I must give thanks after God," solemnly uttered Sprowl. "But where shall I begin?"

"Tell me first about my father: why and how it was that you acted against him as you did."

And then Wesley Sprowl repeated the tale he had briefly outlined to Polk Redlaw, giving every detail in full; but enough has been said to enlighten the reader. It was a terrible tale of revenge and injustice in which an innocent man was made the victim of a villain's plottings, aided by such unscrupulous coadjutors as Sprowl and Jonathan Green.

As the sad incidents of his parent's sorrow and ruin were detailed, Clay Poynter (as we must still call him) bowed his head and wept bitter tears of grief and anguish. Had he glanced toward his companion, he would have seen that " White Crees," the outlaw leader, had bowed his stalwart form, and it shook as if with mortal agony.

"About your being driven from Arkansas," said Sprowl, "I know nothing save that this same man followed you in his hatred for your father; that he had sworn you, too, should die a felon's death. But you fled from him, and it was years before he found you here.

"He saw me also, and knowing that I was poor, tempted me to aid him, as I had done once before. For weeks before he made his appearance openly, he was undermining your reputation by covert hints and innuendoes, that only too easily found holding-ground in the troubled state of the country; and this was increased by your reticence regarding your affairs and previous life.

"I helped him in this, as did Green, Wigan, Redlaw, Dalton and Gibson. Then you were arrested. Sam Gibson and Frank Dalton were bribed to conceal the dies and counterfeit coin in your house, then to swear to the finding it.

" Jonathan Green was bought over, as I was, to swear as he did. For fear one charge should fail, he arranged that of the murder of John Dement, by which name he had made the acquaintance of Neil McGuire, as they both were fellow Masons.

"He made himself popular in the neighborhood by his friendly manner and the freedom with which he spent his money.

"He gave me the diamond cluster-pin that was so well known, and told me what to swear. I was poor; he threatened to denounce me as one of the gang unless I performed his bidding, and I consented. It was hard, though, although you may not believe me.

"You had acted the generous friend to me and mine; had furnished food, clothing and medicine, when I was sick and unable to work; all this you did, and yet I would have sworn away your life!" and for a few moments he remained silent.

"Had it not been for the firmness of Neil McGuire, our plans would have been fully carried out, and that next morning's sun would have shone upon your corpse, as we fully expected. But then you escaped; how, I never learned.

"Meagreson was in Leavenworth awaiting the message that I had promised to send or bring him of your death, but instead it was that you were once more a free man. Still he thought and hoped that you would be taken, and had set the police of the city on the alert for you in case you should go there; but it was useless.

"He was fully disguised, as he had been while here, for as he is now over fifty years of age, his hair is naturally almost snow-white. But he wore his years well, and he was not suspected for other than he seemed.

"You know how I attempted to fire your house—it was that mongrel cur, Polk Redlaw, that tempted me; and that I was captured in the endeavor, I now sincerely thank God! It is one crime the less upon my soul; and He knows that there are enough there already," concluded Sprowl in a broken tone, as he bowed his head, while the hot, scalding tears trickled freely adown his wrinkled cheeks.

There was no affectation about this, as his hearers were fully convinced. He was really moved at the kind and honorable manner in which he had been treated by those whom he had wronged so deeply and terribly.

"And this Meagreson—do you know nothing of his future plans?" at length asked Poynter, looking up.

"Unless he should hear from me, he was to meet me at the 'Twin Points,' Friday night."

"Then you think he will come?"

"I have no doubt of it," was the assured reply. "He will be too anxious to learn the latest news not to come."

"Good! he will probably meet visitors he does not expect," cried Crees.

"That he will! Unless he fails, we will have him at our own terms, and then—"

"And then!" echoed the outlaw.

CHAPTER XI.
FYFFE SOUNDS HIS NOTE.

"HARK!"

It was Poynter who made the exclamation, abruptly checking the outlaw's words. The three men slightly bowed their heads, as if listening intently, while their eyes sought each other's faces. The sound came again.

It was the loud exclamation of a man—such as one would make in driving a refractory yoke of oxen. And yet it could scarcely be that, for the ground surrounding, whence the alarm proceeded, was rough and broken, difficult even for a man to traverse upon foot.

"What is it?" whispered Crees.

"S-sh! Listen."

"Dod-rot y'ur ongainly copperossyty, kain't you walk 'chalk? Gee, thar—gee, you 'tarnel critter! Dod burn ef I don't rouse you up with a saplin'. G'long, now, you creepin' snake!"

A tirade of such adjurations, followed by what sounded like the crack of a whip, and then a strange sort of muffled howl. Such were the noises that aroused the curiosity of the trio, in the little glade.

"Scratch dirt, now, you'd better. 'Tain't much furder, or durned ef I b'lieve we'd git thar to-day. Git up an' git, now, less I'll go ahead an' snip you 'long arter me. How'd thet suit, eh, ole stick-in-the-mud? Shoot at an honest feller ag'in, w'u'd ye? Guess ye won't, no more. Hoop-la!" and then came several more cracks, accompanied by groans and half-choked howls.

"It's Jack," whispered Crees. "Wonder what he's up to?"

"Look!"

As Poynter uttered this exclamation, the bushes parted, and a miserable-looking object broke out into full view. It was a man, but so tattered and begrimed that little else could be guessed. Whether white, black or red, a stranger or an acquaintance, could only be surmised.

His arms were tightly drawn back and secured at the elbows, while a slack withe ran from ankle to ankle. His draggled and matted hair overhung his face, but was not long enough to entirely conceal the existence of a strange freak upon his captor's part. *He was bitted!*

A good-sized stick was secured between his jaws, about two feet in length. To either end of this a supple vine of grape was attached, so that a jerk, right or left, by the driver, would effectually turn the prisoner, if not quite throw him down.

Holding fast to the opposite ends was the grinning Jack Fyffe, who bore a long, supple hickory rod, with which he occasionally "touched up" the captive. Upon his back were two rifles.

"Good Lord, Jack!" cried Poynter, in amazement, at this truly unique "turnout," what under the sun do you mean treating the poor devil that way? Who is he, anyhow?"

"Hellow, square, you thar?" returned the rough borderer, appearing not a whit abashed, giving his captive the twitch necessary to turn his head up the hill, and then adroitly applying the whip, that made him spring nimbly forward. "How air you, anyhow, this mornin'? Kinder fotched along a fri'nd to call on you, sorter permiscuous, like. Git up, thar, *you* critter; step lively, now, an' show the gen'lemen y'ur paces. Hy—ah!"

"For mercy's sake, Jack, let the poor devil loose!"

"Not ef I knows it," retorted Fyffe, coolly; "I hed too much trouble a-gearin' him up, fer thet. An' marcy—the skunk don't know what thet means. *He* didn't hev no marcy onto you nor the ole man, nor likewise on me, when he tried to shoot me, a little back yon."

"Who is it?" queried Crees.

"Why, don't you know? It's Jim Meagreson, John Dement, or Snakey, as *I* call him," declared Fyffe, exultantly.

Poynter stared in amazement, but not to the outlaw leader. With a half-stifled howl of rage and vindictive joy, he drew his knife and leaped forward. Jack Fyffe thought he meant murder, and caught him by the arm.

"Dang it, boss, he's bad enough; but don't butcher him in thet way!"

"Stand off!" yelled Crees, throwing the other violently from him. "Stand off, I say. I am not mad. He is of more use to me living than dead, you fool!"

"All right, then," returned Fyffe, rubbing his shoulder dolefully. "I know thet, but was kinder afeard thet you'd fergit when y'ur mad was up. Thar he is; I turn him over to you fellers an' glad to git shet on him, *I* am."

"'Tis him, Poynter; look!" and Crees held back the captive's head so as to more fully expose the wretch's features.

"It is, indeed," gladly exclaimed Clay, as he beheld the man whom he had been falsely accused of murdering. "And an hour since I would have given ten years of my life if this could have been assured me."

"Wal, square, thar he is, 'thout any o' thet. You're welcome to my shar'."

"But how'd you chance upon him, Jack?"

"Thet's a long yarn—too long fer a feller to spin what hain't had no breakfast," added Fyffe.

"True; I forgot. Go get something and then come up. We may need you," and then, as the borderer hastened down the hill, the young man turned to the captive.

He was in a truly pitiable condition; but those who beheld him had been far too deeply injured by him to indulge in any such feeling. True, they gave him brandy and bathed his head, but it was only to restore him so that they could gain his confession.

He soon revived and stared around at the two men, Sprowl having taken a position out of sight behind the tree, where he had not yet been seen by Meagreson. The men eyed him in silence, but he only vouchsafed them a look of angry defiance.

"Well, James Meagreson," at length said the outlaw leader, "we meet once again!"

"My name is *not* Meagreson, and I don't

know you—never set eyes on you before," sullenly responded the captive.

"Do you know *me*, then?" put in Poynter.

"Know you? Yes; for a vile horse-thief and counterfeiter!"

"Do you mean to say—" began Crees, when he was interrupted by the other.

"I mean to say that I am plain John Dement, an honest trader, and that you shall dearly rue this outrage.

"Bah! that's played out. You may as well own up now, for your accomplice and tool has betrayed you, and exposed all your plots and crimes. If you are obstinate, we will just hand you over to the Vigilance Committee, whose aid you are so fond of invoking, and let them deal with you."

"Am I a fool?" sneered Meagreson. "Don't I know that you dare no more show your face to one of them than to kiss a rattlesnake? The only answer you'd get would be a hempen cord and swinging bough!"

"Now that's nonsense, old man," put in Sprowl. "*You're* the fool. They've got you in a corner, and you may as well come down. Green and the rest of the boys have owned up, and unless you make terms as we did, it'll be all night with you."

"Who's that?" faltered the prisoner, a gray shade settling upon his florid features.

"Sprowl," replied that worthy. "I've told all I know and am going to swear to it, if you are obstinate; and as you very well know, it's enough to hang you a dozen times over."

"The others—"

"I tell you they've 'peached, and you're a spotted man, if these gentlemen are only a mind to press the matter," glibly said Sprowl.

A deep groan was his only answer, as Meagreson fell forward, his form trembling like a leaf.

"Let him be, Poynter," said Crees, "and when he thinks it all over, he'll see that it's of no use holding out further. Here comes Fyffe."

"Hellow, what you fellows bin a-doin' to my hoss?" cried that worthy, as he leisurely strolled up the hill, wiping his greasy mouth upon his shirt-sleeve, and smacking his lips.

"Never mind now, Jack," interrupted Poynter. "He's thinking."

"Yas; needs it, I reckon. While y'ur hand's in, jest think a leetle how all-fired nigh you come to killin' a feller-critter-man. Sp'ilt my ha'r, anyhow," at the same time tugging at a shaggy lock that grew beside his ear, trying to bring it before his eyes. "See thar."

It did indeed look as though a bullet had cut a jagged passage through it, as he had hinted. Then Poynter seated himself beneath the tree, motioning Jack to do the same, saying:

"There's nothing else just now, Fyffe; sit down and tell us how you chanced upon this fellow, and all about it."

"Don't care 'f I do, square," quoth Jack, gnawing off a huge mouthful of "niggerhead," and then passing the plug to Sprowl. "Don't chaw, b'lieve?"

"No."

"I do. Wal, I allus war fond o' tellin' stories. Mam, she used to dress my trowsers with her ol' slipper purty nigh the hull time, 'cause of this habit o' mine; but, Lord, thet didn't do no good. Only driv' it back ag'in, like. But dad, he *was* a yarner, now I tell you! I kedn't hold a kendle to him when he'd got a good streak on, but thet's nyther hyar nor thar.

"When I 'gun winkin' this daylight, airly, I got up an' begun sorter swoopin' 'round fer grub. But blamed the bit could I find, 'cept some wenzun, an' I swore I'd hev none o' thet. Fact is, my appertite is sorter delacut, like, an' won't b'ar plain grub, like you bigger fellers.

"So, as I went down to the crick fer a drink, I see'd lots o' gre't big turkey-tracks in the mud, toes a-p'intin' downarts; an' so I jest shoulders shooter an' shakes moccasin sorter lively, 'cause I'd made up my mind to hev a gobbler fer breakfust, *an'* nothin' shorter.

"But I trailed them dratted birds so fur thet I'd e'ena'most gi'n up all hups o' drappin' one, an' hed 'bout made up my mind thet wenzun was a heap better, enyhow, when I sot blinkers on as fine a strutter as ever gobbled to a hen. Up goes my gun, slip goes my fut, an' down I rolls inter the crick, while the dratted bird flops off through the bushes.

"*Didn't* I cuss some, sorter, as I got out? Mebbe not; 'tany rate, off I put ag'in arter thet turkey, fer I swore I'd hev it ef it tuck all day. No 'tarnal two-legged bird sh'u'd fool me like thet, not by no manner o' means, ef I knowed myself, an' I rayther thunk I did. So on I splurges, lickety-split.

"But I stopped ag'in, mighty sudden, though 'twa'n't a turkey I see'd. It was a man kinder strollin' along, fer his health, I reckon, an' he pulled up, too. Thar we stud, a-gawpin' at each other like looneys, when he spluttered out sunkthin' thet kinder smelled o' brimstone, and then took to his heels like the devil was arter him.

"An' ef *he* wasn't, I was, 'cause I never yet see'd a feller thet run, 'thout takin' arter him jest like blazes. It's a kinder 'farmity like, I reckon; anyhow it's a fact. Wal, he put an' I put, jest a-scratchin' dirt an' a-kickin' up the leaves the beatinest kind you ever did hyar tell on.

"I'm purty hefty on the run, as ye know, but blamed ef he wasn't mighty nigh my master. But I'd never say die till the bellers clean bu'sted, an' at last he jumped for kiver, a-swingin' his shooter mighty keerless like. I did ditto, an' thar we war. I sorter grinned, 'cause it 'minded me of ol' times when ha'r went wild.

"But then I peeked out, mighty keerful like, 'cause I didn't want another hole in my brush-patch overly much, when I hope I may never see the back o' my neck, ef thar he wasn't a-streakin' it through the woods, his coat-tails a-streamin' out wuss'n the tag eend to a comet. Lord, wasn't I gritty then? Mebbe not!

"I jest set my grinders like a clamp, pulled the slouch furder on my head an' then set ol' toad-smashers to work. The ground jest fa'rly smoked about me, I run so fast, and I overhauled ol' smarty like fun. He peeked 'round an' see'd it, then whirled 'round to'rds me, yellin' out he'd shoot fer shore.

"But my Ebenezer was up like a mice, an' I kept on, wild fer bitin' an' gougin'. The dratted imp did shoot shore enough, but it jest clipped my ha'r a leetle, an' then I downed him,

I was mad at the feller's impedence in burnin' powder when I was jest in fun, all the time, an' drawed my knife to finish up the job.

"I had her raised all ready, when I caught his eye, an' helt my han'. I knowed him in a minute, though he'd changed a heap sence we met last. I knowed how tickled the ol' man 'uld be, ef he see'd him, 'cause he kinder 'lowed he kicked the bucket long ago.

"But thar he was, an' I 'tarmined to fotch him inter camp. So I started, but the bugger tried to run onc't or twic't, an' so I thought I'd see how he'd work in a single gear. He cut up rusty a leetle, an' n'arly nipped off my thumb, the onmannerly brute; but when I once got him fa'rly bitted he done purty well, barrin' the kickin' an' stumblin'," concluded Fyffe, with a long-drawn yawn.

"It'll turn out the best day's work you ever done, Fyffe," said Crees, extending his hand.

"And I will not forget it very soon, either, old fellow," warmly added Poynter.

"Wal, ef so be you fellers is satisfied, I'm shore I be," grunted Jack, lying back upon the grass.

"But what do you think I'd best do next, Mr. Crees?" asked Poynter, after a slight pause, a little anxiously. "I think, with Sprowl's evidence, here, I need not hesitate about showing myself openly once more."

"You have a good deal to work against down there yet, and I think you'd best wait a little, and see what we can get out of our friend, yonder," responded Crees, thoughtfully.

"Well, I suppose I must, though it's hard to be lying idle when such charges are hanging over me," sighed Poynter.

CHAPTER XII.
POYNTER FINDS SOMETHING.

It was in the afternoon of the same day which Fyffe had so signalized by his turkey-hunt. The prisoner, James Meagreson, was occupying the same position in which Sprowl had done penance some hours before. He had been left here by his captors to ponder upon his situation and reflect as to which should be his future course, whether to persist in his denials or acknowledge defeat and submit to his triumphant enemies with such grace as he could muster.

In the mean time the three friends were gathered together, smoking or conversing idly, or buried deep in thought. Presently Jack Fyffe lay back, dropped his pipe, and then his stertorous breathing announced that he was in a deep, sound slumber.

The remainder of the band had either long since done the same, or went off upon business of their own; the scouts sent out having reported that all was quiet among the Vigilantes, those worthies having disbanded and returned to their daily occupations, no doubt highly edified by their midnight wild-goose chase.

Save the regular sentinels, none appeared to be upon the alert excepting Poynter and Crees. The latter was covertly but intently regarding his younger companion with a strange, faraway look in his deep-black eyes, while an unconscious sigh would now and then heave up from his massive chest, as if engendered by some painful memory of bygone days.

Poynter suddenly aroused himself, and glancing hastily around, uttered:

"Why, where's Sprowl?"

"Yonder," returned Crees, pointing to the ragged form of the man inquired after, lying under a bush, sleeping. "Poor devil, his last night was a hard one."

"True, but he had no one to thank for it save himself. However, I have some hopes of him yet. He is not *all* bad, and for the sake of his family I am willing to lend him a helping hand. His wife, poor thing, has seen hard times of late years. The entire support of the family, and of this shiftless, lazy brute into the bargain, has fallen upon her. And she is a perfect lady, too, for all she's uneducated. It's strange what choices women will make sometimes!" exclaimed Poynter.

The outlaw leader only grunted, "Just so."

"But that isn't what I wanted to talk to you about just now. You have several times promised to tell me your story, and why not fulfill it now? 'Tis as well to wait longer."

"You are right, and I will do so; although I had intended to wait until after Meagreson had acknowledged his guilt. But what Sprowl has said is enough," slowly replied Crees, passing a hand across his brow, as if to chase away some painful reflection.

"But I have not heard him mention your name?" cried Poynter, in surprise.

"Yes, you have heard him tell my whole story, or nearly so. Henry Duaber, *my son*, have you no greeting for *your father?*"

"Son—father!" faltered the young man, gazing in bewilderment upon the outlaw leader, at this strange appeal.

"Your father, Henry," continued the elder man, in a choked tone; "can you not believe me?"

"But my father was—is dead!"

"No, not dead—only in name; he escaped with life. I am your father. By your dead mother—by my sainted wife, boy, I swear it!" solemnly said Crees.

"Is it—can it be true? I will believe it—father!" brokenly exclaimed the young man, bending forward to meet the proffered embrace.

It was a holy scene, this strange meeting of long-parted kindred; and their tears were mingled together, tears such as strong men need not be ashamed to shed. They were deeply affected, as well they might be, and when the first gush of emotion had passed, they sat beside each other, hand clasped in hand, gazing kindly and affectionately at each other.

"It is strange—passing strange!" at length uttered Henry (as we must now call him, Clay Poynter no longer). "More like a romance than any thing in real everyday life. I have mourned you as dead since my childhood, and now find you my kindest friend, while I still thought you a stranger. How long since you first recognized me?"

"Not until to-day, although your story awoke strange fancies, it was so like mine; but I, too, thought you were dead, I had heard so, and saw what purported to be your grave."

"My grave!"

"Yes. They told me you had died at nearly the same time with your mother. Why, I know not. It could not have been from malice, for they knew me not. I was a stranger in my native home."

"But you—how were we deceived, and why did you not tell us of your escape, and our dear one might still have been alive?"

"Listen, and I will tell you all," replied James Duaber, in broken tones. "It is a sad, sad story of cruel wrong and sorrow; but I was the victim—I and mine! You know the first, or sufficiently well as to render a *resume* unnecessary. But it was James Meagreson—the wretch yonder—who caused it all for revenge, because your mother chose me in preference to him.

"A man named Frank Soutar was confined in the same apartment with me, upon a charge identical with the one for which I was to suffer; but as he acknowledged to me, deeming me of the same gang, he was guilty. The mob knew nothing of his having been changed to my cell, as it had only been done that same day, and when they broke open the doors in the dead of night, he was seized for me in the confusion and darkness, while I hid beneath the pallet.

"And the error was never discovered by the mob: they hung him, thinking they were doing as they had been bribed by Meagreson, who took that way to insure my death, fearing lest I should eventually escape his revenge if he left the law to decide. He was hung, but I took advantage of the open door to flee, and during the excitement, managed to effect my escape unmolested.

"A stanch friend of mine, Jack Fyffe, yonder —who was also under the ban, and in hiding—managed to secure his two horses, and upon them we rapidly fled the country. He had joined the mob with the hope of assisting me to escape, and he alone discovered the error, in time to return and assist me.

"We rode hard all that night, and lay hid at day, for we feared that the error would be discovered in the morning, at least, and then the hounds would be hot upon our trail. We traveled in this way until out of the State, and far into the wilds of Arkansas. But even then we did not feel secure, and thought it best to lie concealed until the storm had blown over.

"Still, I wrote, and managed to post two letters to my wife, telling of my safety, and that I would soon return to remove her and you to our new refuge. Besides this, I counted upon her knowing of my escape, else I would have dared all to have seen her.

"So I waited for six months and then was upon my way back when I met a man who had just come through there. He did not know us, and I questioned him closely. Then it was that I learned of her death, and that you, too, had died. I did not doubt its entire truth, and in my wretchedness I plunged into crimes and dissipation to drown reflection.

"For years this went on, until a time came when I felt driven to return to the graves of my dead. No one knew me: I was a stranger in my native home, I had changed so, and saw where my wife lay, and what they said was your last resting-place. Then I went back again to the old life, and lived it until I met with you.

"Although I knew you not—you had changed your name, and I did not recognize the little boy in the stalwart, handsome man—I felt drawn toward you. And now that you know how sinful I have been, will you still take me by the hand and say, father? It is blackened, but there is no blood upon it."

"Father!" cried Henry, once more embracing the outlaw leader. "What matters it now? You leave this life, and we will be all in all to each other from now henceforth!"

"Thunder 'n' lightnin'! jest look at Snakey!" yelled out Jack Fyffe, as he sprung to his feet before them and wildly pointed up the hill.

And there was good cause for his excitement.

During the respite afforded by his captors, Meagreson had not been idle after the first few minutes. His was not a mind to despair for any length of time, and although greatly astounded at the unexpected meeting with a man whom he had thought long since numbered with the dead, his mind speedily resumed its wonted activity, and he thought but of escape.

Minute after minute he toiled and twisted at the thongs that secured him to the tree, until they rolled up into hours. The skin and flesh were terribly abraded, yet he did not heed the pain. Every instant he expected the return of his enemies, to receive the decision he might have arrived at, when in all probability the progress he had already made would be discovered.

Little by little he worked the cords loose, until one of his hands slipped from the noose. It was with the greatest difficulty that he restrained the shout of exultation that arose to his lips; but he did so, and then his other hand was free.

With his hands once free, it was but the work of a minute for the captive to release the rest of his body, and he stepped from the tree, a free man once more. His keen eyes glanced hurriedly around, and in the one look, took in every chance, both for and against his escape.

If he started to flee upon foot, he would, to an almost dead certainty, be discovered and overtaken, as his frame was stiff and weary. Besides, under cover of the one little clump in which he now stood, the entire hillside was fully exposed to the view of the three men below.

But his eye glittered, and the old cold gray look settled upon his face, as his gaze fell upon the form of a horse, all ready equipped for the road, standing carelessly hitched to a pendent bough. If he could once reach that, he felt that escape was assured.

Gathering all his faculties and straining every nerve, Meagreson made a wild bound from his covert and dashed swiftly down the hillside toward the horse. And had it not been for the watchful eyes of Jack Fyffe, no doubt he would have succeeded, perfectly. But the borderer's shout brought both father and son to their feet, pistol in hand.

"After him, Jack—Henry!" yelled the outlaw leader, "don't shoot—take him alive," but as he spoke, the revolvers of his companions were discharged.

Discharged, but the only perceptible result was a quicker and longer bound upon the fugitive's part.

"Take him, boys; for God's sake don't let him get free! You men on guard—stop that horse!" screamed the chief, as the trio bounded forward with headlong speed.

The fugitive gained the rearing horse in safety, tearing the bridle-reins loose, leaped into the saddle, and with a wild yell, darted away, waving his hand in defiance. And to the great chagrin of his enemies, he disappeared in triumph among the trees.

But their speed was suddenly checked, and for a moment they paused, glancing at each other. Their ears had caught a clear challenge to halt, closely followed by a single whip-like crack; then a wild shriek as of a human being in mortal agony, the quick trampling of hoofs, and then all was still.

As they once more pressed forward in painful suspense, a low, unearthly groan sounded from the spot whence the shot had come. Bursting through the bushes, the quartette—for Sprowl had also joined them—beheld a terrible sight.

A man—one of the outlaw guards—was coolly recharging his rifle, with his gaze bent upon a bleeding form before him. There, pale and ghastly, lay the form of James Meagreson; not dead, but apparently dying. The lower portion of his body lay still and motionless, but his head and shoulders writhed to and fro, while his arms were tossed wildly about, in the intensity of his agony.

The fatal missile had entered his stomach, and passing through, had broken his back.

The men did not attempt to remove him or to bandage his wound; they saw that such a course would only be inflicting useless torment upon him, that his time had come; his life slowly ebbing away with the fast-fleeting moments. Two of them knelt beside his head, and kept him from hastening his end by the useless struggles.

James Duaber spoke to him kindly, imploring him to confess before he died, but his only answer was bitter revilings and curses, the fearful words coming as they did from lips fast chilling in the embrace of death, caused even those strong men to turn aside with a shudder.

And thus he died, still reckless and defiant—a fitting end for his long and sinful life. There were grave faces that surrounded him, as breath went out, but no tears, no grief at his tragic end. Their injuries had been far too deep.

By this time the majority of the troop had collected, alarmed by the disturbance, and a number of them were detailed by their chief to prepare a grave for the dead man. It was soon completed, and the corpse was quietly lowered into the bark-lined pit; then the damp mold covered him forever from mortal ken. There was no whispered prayer, no murmured blessing over the unhallowed grave, and nothing but the long, narrow mound remained to show where the unfortunate being had been laid for his last long sleeping-place.

Unloved he had lived, and unloved he had died. Poor James Meagreson.

CHAPTER XIII.

DEATH AMID JOY.

WHEN we raise the curtain once more upon our characters, it is after the lapse of three months. A quarter of a year, that has not been uneventful to those in whom we are interested; but we cannot linger upon them. A brief glance at the leading episodes is all.

The unfortunate death of James Meagreson changed the entire plans of the outlawed couple—father and son. But first of all James Duaber announced to his followers his intention of leaving them, and for the future leading an honest life.

Some of them murmured, but their chief was too highly estemed and respected for them to raise any serious opposition. Some few of their number joined him in his resolve, but the majority determined to continue on; the wild, free life having charms they could not resist. But it was agreed to leave the neighborhood, and ply their calling elsewhere.

So their attention was only turned to the vindication of Henry Duaber's honor, as the father was totally unknown to the settlers, and the charges brought against him had long since passed into oblivion. Their first move was to secretly abduct Frank Dalton, and when he was confronted with Wesley Sprowl, and found that his perjury had been discovered, he promised to make restitution, as far as lay in his power at any time he was called upon.

Thus prepared, Henry Duaber boldly returned to the settlement, where he was once more arrested by the excited Vigilance Committee. His trial came off in good time, and thanks to the candor of his witnesses, he was triumphantly acquitted.

None were more cordial and sincere in their congratulations than Neil McGuire and "Honest Jim" Henderson, who declared his bar was free to everybody upon the joyous occasion.

There was some talk about giving the perjured witnesses a taste of "birch law," but, thanks to the firm opposition of Henry and others, it was not carried into effect. There was one familiar face missing among the crowd, but none regretted this fact. Polk Redlaw was not in the best of odor among his *quondam* associates, and did not make his appearance.

The "big house" was reopened, and old Aunt Eunice in her glory once more, never tiring of dwelling upon the prominent part *she* had played in the late events. Henry met with no further opposition from the father of Nora, and matters progressed finely between the young couple, and at the same time no less rapidly.

Henry was an ardent suitor, and pleaded his case so well that the "fatal day" was set; and when we reopen our chronicle it had arrived. Great preparations had been made, and although the weather was somewhat cool, it was decided to have a grand barbecue and dance by moonlight in the open air.

Upon the summit of a little knoll was a sort of pavilion, erected for the dancing. The floor was composed of puncheons, the flat side uppermost, rudely dressed with an ax. Seats of the same were ranged around the sides, each end resting upon a block of wood. At one extremity projecting beyond the platform, a stand was erected for the musicians, of whom there were three already present.

Busy preparations were going on a little distance from the pavilion, for the "barbecue;" in full view, but far enough away to avoid inconvenience from the smoke, deer and hogs were being prepared for the spit—cattle were by far too valuable for that purpose—while turkey, ducks, prairie-chickens and smaller game were being roasted at the house. These minor items were to be furnished by the guests, who were each expected to " bring something."

It was early yet, but "out West" that is the fashion, and several parties had already arrived, although too few to begin dancing. Then the guests began to drop in more frequently; singly, in couples, or small parties of several; the ladies hastening to the cabin to make any little arrangement of their finery, while their cavaliers unsaddled the horses, securing them to the surrounding trees, placing fodder before them, and then joining the company already gathered at the pavilion.

Presently the scraping and tuning of violins broke the spell, and seemed to dissipate the restraint that surrounded all parties. The groups began to mingle and converse more freely; the tap of some dainty foot to be heard as it kept unconscious time to the music; the confused request and murmured consent to dance; then the order, " Choose your pardners, boys!" the sets were formed, and Henry, with Nora, led off.

The fun waxed fast and furious, the din increased, and the sets appeared mixed in inextricable confusion, the clatter of heavy-soled, horse-hide boots, the lighter fall of a more dainty foot, the rustle of dresses and shuffle of moccasins, with now and then a gay burst of laughter at some unlucky wight who makes a ludicrous blunder; or a stentorian shout from some half-wild borderer as he grows excited: mixed and intermingled with the music, more loud than melodious, while above all soars the clear voice of the "caller-off."

The picture is homely, we grant you, but it is pleasant, nevertheless, and it would be hard indeed to find a fashionable gathering that contains so little alloy of envy, pain and hypocrisy as this little congregation of rude, unpolished, but kind and open-hearted people. Rough and unlettered they may be, but their hospitality shames that of many a more pretentious class; while it would indeed be hard to find a truer or a more generous heart than those that beat under a deer-skin hunting-shirt, or homespun dress of linsey-woolsey.

Occasionally during the figure "promenade all," the toe of some clumsy swain, or perchance that of his rosy lassie, would catch fast in some crevice or protuberance between the rudely-joined puncheons, that cast them with violence to the floor. The next couple being too close and under great headway, would follow suit, and a mass of writhing, struggling humanity form a prostrate heap upon the floor.

Oh! what a burst of laughter would then ascend from hearty lungs, echoing through the woods from grove to grove, arousing the feathered songsters from their nests, causing them to chirp and twitter, no doubt wondering what possessed the people at that unseasonable hour.

Then Jack Fyffe—who did not dance—caused a renewed burst of merriment by seating himself upon one end of an unusually refractory slab, to hold it in its proper place, as he said. And there he sat, as solemn as a judge, smoking his pipe complacently, as though a crowd of gay dancers were not whirling all about him, until the gathering broke up for supper.

And such a supper! More fit to be likened to a bounteous dinner, served up for a regiment of half-famished, war-worn soldiers The long tables, manufactured from slabs of rudely-hewn wood, and supported by stakes probably furnished from the limbs of the same tree, were piled almost to overflowing with game and pastry.

Such saddles and haunches of venison; delicious buffalo-humps and pickled tongues—the proceeds of an extended hunt, for this especial occasion—the wild turkey, lusciously brown and tempting, almost bursting with the rich dressing; the prairie-chicken and pheasant, quail and snipe; even down to the huge ",black-bird pot-pie."

Then the appetizing pastry and preserves, the results of that same season's "berry-hunting;" the honey, from that as clear and limpid as amber, to the dark and strong-flavored "bee-bread"—the varicolored comb piled in great stacks.

And the strong, fragrant coffee, sweetened with honey and tempered with the thick, golden cream; the highly-prized tiny cups of "real boughten tea," mingled with stronger draughts for those so inclined, of "corn-whisky" and crab-apple cider.

All this, to say nothing of the barbecued game, which is in great demand from the very novelty of its cooking—I could not tell you one tithe of the good things that were there; the very sight of such abundance seeming enough to banish one's appetite for a fortnight to come.

Henry and Nora were the gayest of the gay, even among that happy crowd, and kept those surrounding them in the highest glee with their witticism and repartee. But they left the table among the first, and strolled back toward the pavilion.

Jack Fyffe fidgeted around for a few moments and then hastily followed after, announcing his approach with a sonorous cough, that startled the young couple into turning around.

"Beg pardin, square," apologetically began the borderer "but p'r'aps you'd better be on y'ur guard, like."

"Why so, Josh?—what do you mean?" asked Henry.

"Jest take a squint over yander, an' mebbe you'll see."

Duaber glanced in the direction indicated, and a hot flush passed over his face as he noticed the tall, dark form of Polk Redlaw leaning against a tree, apparently deeply absorbed in thought. But had they been a little closer, a snakelike look would have been seen from beneath the slouched hat, fixed vindictively upon them, while one of the hands that rested across his bosom fiercely gripped the haft of a long, keen knife, hidden within his shirt. "He here!"

"Never mind, Henry, let him go," nervously whispered Nora, "he can't hurt you now."

"If he keeps his distance I will not molest him," answered Henry. "Besides, I do not believe he is armed. Do you see any, Jack?"

"No, but that don't signify," grunted that worthy. "A snake don't show its teeth till it goes to strike, an' *he's* a copperhead, *he* is."

"Well, I'll watch him," and the young couple turned away, while Jack, his mind relieved by delivering the warning, repaired to the table to indulge in another meal.

But in five minutes more Henry had totally forgotten the warning, and had thoughts only for Nora. Fortunately she was not so oblivious, and hearing a slight noise behind them turned suddenly, just in time to behold the crouching form of the mongrel, as he uplifted his heavy knife.

Her shriek startled Duaber, and he quickly turned, in the nick of time, to nimbly avoid his enemy's rush, adroitly tripping him with one foot, while he delivered a lightning-like blow with his right fist, full upon the dastard's neck, that hurled him headlong to the ground as if he had been shot. Before the affray could go any further, the combatants were surrounded and Redlaw disarmed, being rather roughly handled by Jack Fyffe, who finally ended by kicking him from the grounds.

In a short time the incident was forgotten by the majority, and the dancing once more resumed. But Jack did not occupy his old position, and when he again appeared he was fully armed, a rifle in hand and revolver at his waist. Neither did he enter the pavilion, but stationed himself at a little distance, beside a tree, where his form was so blended with the shadows that at a score yards distant it was not visible. So another hour passed away, and he obstinately retained his post, heedless of fatigue.

Suddenly he uttered a low grunt, and crouched forward, half-raising his rifle, while the faint click told of its being cocked. A dim, shadow-like form had caught his roving glance, and upon it his every attention was now centered. Twice the long barrel rose to his cheek, and as often was it lowered, while his head craned forward as if in doubt.

Just then the music ceased, at the words, "Promenade all—to your seats!" and the dancers separated. Jack Fyffe gave vent to a startling yell, and quickly raising his rifle, discharged it with an instantaneous aim.

The wild cry that followed told how true had been his aim; but it was duplicated. Quick as had been his motion, another flash had streamed out upon the darkness, from one spot at which he had aimed, and *two* cries were mingled with the reverberating echoes, and then came a dull, heavy fall upon the floor of the pavilion.

Jack did not glance toward the latter, but with an angry howl, more like that of a famished wild beast than a man, leaped forward toward the spot from whence had come the secret shot. A dark form lay there, motionless and silent, but he heeded not that. One by one the chambers of his revolver were emptied, and then he spurned from him with his foot the dead and mangled form of the mongrel assassin, Polk Redlaw.

In the pavilion a pale and horrified group were gathered, some bending over the bleeding, senseless form of Henry Duaber, while others attended to the fainting girl who was so soon to have become his bride. Heads were gravely shaken in answer to inquiring looks; their decision was that the young man would never speak again.

He breathed faintly, but each respiration seemed as if it would be his last. The blood slowly oozed from a ghastly wound upon his head, and they said that his brain had been pierced.

But we are happy to be enabled to state that they were greatly mistaken; had it been true, it would have made too sorrowful an ending to our story—one that the reader might well grumble at; for there had been no marriage as yet, and what is a novel without that?

In fact, he recovered his senses long before Nora did, and when his wound was washed, it was found that the bullet had only cut a deep gash upon his head, merely stunning him for the time being. When he had once convinced Nora that he was really unharmed, he declared he only had a slight headache, and made the assertion good by carrying out the original programme, and heroically passing the trying ordeal of changing the young lady into Mrs. Nora Duaber, that same night.

The dance was broken up by this catastrophe, and while no one expressed pity for the dead man, he was reverently buried, before another sun shone. Nora knew nothing of this at the time, and her joy was unclouded, for more reasons than one.

And now we must leave them, with only a few parting words.

The young couple duly entered the "big house," where, with Aunt Eunice for a house keeper, they led a peaceful, happy life. A few years since, James Duaber died, loved and respected by all who knew him; the fact of his old reckless life having never transpired, the secret being safe between the three.

Wesley Sprowl still lives, and is in moderately comfortable circumstances, thanks to the generosity with which Henry Duaber fulfilled his promise. He is not rich, and never will be; his disposition prevents that. But his sad and long-suffering wife has greatly changed for the better we are glad to state.

And worthy Jack Fyffe, although now well along in years, is still hale and hearty; can handle his heavy rifle with sufficient precision to keep the larder well supplied with small game, and takes great delight in teaching the little Duabers how to shoot, swim and ride. He and "Honest Jim" Henderson are great cronies, often sitting for hours over their glasses and pipes, vying with each other in their stories of "when I was young." To listen for a while, one would be strongly tempted to believe that "Sindbad the Sailor," "Robinson Crusoe" or the worthy "Baron Munchausen" had returned to life, and inhabited the shapes of "the venerable story-tellers."

THE END.

32 Octavo Pages. **BEADLE'S BOY'S LIBRARY.** **Price, Five Cents.**

ISSUED EVERY SATURDAY.

1 **Deerhunter**, the Boy Scout of the Great North Woods. By Oll Coomes.
2 **Buffalo Bill**, from Boyhood to Manhood. By Col. Prentiss Ingraham.
3 **Kit Carson**, King of Guides. By Albert W. Aiken.
4 **Gordon Lillie**, the Boy-Interpreter of the Pawnees. By Major. H. B. Stoddard.
5 **Bruin Adams**, Old Grizzly's Boy Pard. By Colonel Prentiss Ingraham.
6 **Deadwood Dick as a Boy.** By Edward L. Wheeler.
7 **Wild Bill**, the Pistol Prince. By Colonel Prentiss Ingraham.
8 **The Prairie Ranch.** By Joseph E. Badger, Jr.
9 **Roving Joe:** The History of a "Border Boy." By A. H. Post.
10 **Texas Jack**, the Mustang King. By Colonel Prentiss Ingraham.
11 **Charley Skylark.** A Story of School-day Scrapes and College Capers. By Major H. B. Stoddard.
12 **Mariposa Marsh.** By Joseph E. Badger, Jr.
13 **Roving Ben.** By John J. Marshall.
14 **Spring Steel**, King of the Bush. By J. E. Badger, Jr.
15 **Wide-Awake George**, the Boy Pioneer. By Edward Willett
16 **The Boy Wizard.** By Barry Ringgold.
17 **Peter Peppergrass**, the Greenhorn from Gotham. By Noah Nuff.
18 **Adrift on the Prairie, and Amateur Hunters on the Buffalo Range.** By Oll Coomes.
19 **The Fortune Hunter;** or, Roving Joe as Miner, Cowboy, Trapper and Hunter. By A. H. Post.
20 **Trapper Tom**, the Wood Imp. By T. C. Harbaugh.
21 **Yellow Hair**, the Boy Chief of the Pawnees. By Col. Prentiss Ingraham.
22 **The Snow Trail.** By T. C. Harbaugh.
23 **Old Grizzly Adams**, the Bear Tamer. By Dr. Frank Powell.
24 **Woods and Waters.** By Capt. Frederick Whittaker.
25 **A Rolling Stone:** Incidents in the Career on Sea and Land of Col. Prentiss Ingraham. By Wm. R. Eyster.
26 **Red River Rovers.** By C. Dunning Clark.
27 **Plaza and Plain;** or, Wild Adventures of "Buckskin Sam," (Maj. Sam. S. Hall.) By Col. P. Ingraham.
28 **The Sword Prince.** The Romantic Life of Col. Monstery. By Capt. Frederick Whittaker.
29 **Snow-Shoe Tom.** By T. C. Harbaugh.
30 **Paul de Lacy**, the French Beast Charmer. By C. Dunning Clark.
31 **Round the Camp Fire.** By Joseph E. Badger, Jr.
32 **White Beaver**, the Indian Medicine Chief. By Col. Prentiss Ingraham.
33 **The Boy Crusader.** By Capt. Fred. Whittaker.
34 **The Chase of the Great White Stag, and, Camp and Canoe.** By C. Dunning Clark.
35 **Old Tar Knuckle** and His Boy Chums. By R. Starbuck.
36 **The Dashing Dragoon;** or, The Story of Gen. George A. Custer. By Capt. Fred. Whittaker.
37 **Night-Hawk George.** By Col. Prentiss Ingraham.
38 **The Boy Exiles of Siberia.** By T. C. Harbaugh.
39 **The Young Bear Hunters.** By Morris Redwing.
40 **Smart Sim**, the Lad with a Level Head. By Edward Willett.
41 **The Settler's Son.** By Edward S. Ellis.
42 **Walt Ferguson's Cruise.** By C. Dunning Clark.
43 **Rifle and Revolver.** By Capt. Fred. Whittaker.

44 **The Lost Boy Whalers.** By T. C. Harbaugh.
45 **Bronco Billy**, the Saddle Prince. By Col. Ingraham.
46 **Dick, the Stowaway.** By Charles Morris.
47 **The Colorado Boys;** or, Life on an Indigo Plantation. By Joseph E. Badger, Jr.
48 **The Pampas Hunters;** or, New York Boys in Buenos Ayres. By T. C. Harbaugh.
49 **The Adventurous Life of Nebraska Charlie.** By Col. Prentiss Ingraham.
50 **Jack, Harry and Tom**, the Three Champion Brothers. By Capt. Fred. Whittaker.
51 **The Young Land-Lubber.** By C. Dunning Clark.
52 **The Boy Detectives.** By T. C. Harbaugh.
53 **Honest Harry;** or, The Country Boy Adrift in the City. By Charles Morris.
54 **California Joe**, the Mysterious Plainsman. By Col. Prentiss Ingraham.
55 **Tip Tressel**, the Floater. By Edward Willett.
56 **The Snow Hunters;** or, Winter in the Woods. By Barry de Forrest.
57 **Harry Somers**, the Sailor Boy Magician. By S. W. Pearce.
58 **The Adventurous Life of Captain Jack**, the Border Boy. By Col. Prentiss Ingraham.
59 **Lame Tim**, the Mule Boy of the Mines. By Charles Morris.
60 **The Young Trail Hunters;** or, New York Boys in Grizzly Land. By T. C. Harbaugh.
61 **The Tiger Hunters;** or, The Colorado Boys in Elephant Land. By Joseph E. Badger, Jr.
62 **Doctor Carver**, the "Evil Spirit" of the Plains. By Col. Prentiss Ingraham.
63 **Black Horse Bill**, the Bandit Wrecker. By Roger Starbuck.
64 **Young Dick Talbot;** or, A Boys Rough and Tumble Fight from New York to California. By A. W. Aiken.
65 **The Boy Pilot;** or, The Island Wrecker. By Col. Prentiss Ingraham.
66 **The Desert Rovers;** or, Stowaway Dick Among the Arabs. By Charles Morris.
67 **Texas Charlie**, the Boy Ranger. By Col. Prentiss Ingraham.
68 **Little Rifle;** or, The Young Fur Hunters. By Captain "Bruin" Adams.
69 **The Young Nihilist;** or, A Yankee Boy Among the Russians. By Charles Morris.
70 **Pony the Cowboy;** or, The Young Marshall's Raid. By Major H. B. Stoddard, Ex-Scout.
71 **Ruff Robsart and His Bear.** By Captain "Bruin" Adams.
72 **The Ice Elephant.** By Capt. Frederick Whittaker.
73 **The Young Moose-Hunters.** By William H. Manning.
74 **The Boy Coral-Fishers.** By Roger Starbuck.
75 **Revolver Billy**, the Boy Ranger of Texas. By Col. Prentiss Ingraham.
76 **The Condor Killers.** By T. C. Harbaugh.
77 **Lud Lionheels**, the Young Tiger Fighter. By Roger Starbuck.
78 **Flatboat Fred.** By Edward Willett.
79 **Boone, the Hunter.** By Captain F. Whittaker.

Beadle's Boy's Library is for sale by all Newsdealers, five cents per copy, or sent by mail on receipt of six cents each.

BEADLE AND ADAMS, Publishers,
98 William Street, New York

32 Octavo Pages. BEADLE'S BOY'S LIBRARY. **Price, Five Cents**

ISSUED EVERY SATURDAY.

80 **Kentucky Ben,** the Long Rifle of the Cascades. By Roger Starbuck.
81 **The Kit Carson Club.** By T. C. Harbaugh.
82 **Little Buck,** the Boy Guide. By Barry Ringgold.
83 **Pony Bob** the Reckless Rider of the Rockies. By Col. Prentiss Ingraham.
84 **Captain Fly-by-Night.** By Joseph E. Badger, Jr.
85 **Captain Ralph,** the Young Explorer. By C. Dunning Clark.
86 **Little Dan Rocks.** By Morris Redwing.
87 **The Menagerie Hunters.** By Maj. H. Grenville.
88 **The Boy Tramps;** or, Life Among the Gipsies. By J. M. Hoffman.
89 **'Longshore Life.** By C. D. Clark.
90 **Roving Rifle,** Custer's Little Scout. By T. C. Harbaugh.
91 **Oregon Josh,** the Wizard Rifle. By Roger Starbuck.
92 **Hurricane Kit.** By A. F. Holt.
93 **Jumping Jake,** the Colorado Circus Boy. By Bryant Bainbridge.
94 **Sam Spence,** the Broadhorn Boy. By Ed. Willett.
95 **Moscow to Siberia;** or, A Yankee Boy to the Rescue. By Charles Morris.
96 **Fighting Fred;** or, The Castaways of Grizzly Camp. By T. C. Harbaugh.
97 **Cruise of the Flyaway;** or, Yankee Boys in Ceylon. By C. Dunning Clark.
98 **The Boy Vigilantes;** or, King Cole and His Band. By Maj. H. B. Stoddard.
99 **The White Tigers;** or, Silver Rifle, the Girl Tracker of Lake Superior. By Capt. Charles Howard.
100 **The Snow-Shoe Trail;** or, The Forest Desperadoes. By St. George Rathbone.
101 **Mariano,** the Ottawa Girl; or, The Mysterious Canoe. By Edward S. Ellis.
102 **The Flyaway Afloat;** or, Yankee Boys 'Round the World. By C. Dunning Clark.
103 **Pat Mulloney's Adventures;** or, Silver Tongue the Dacotah Queen. By C. L. Edwards.
104 **The Boy Prospector;** or, The Secret of the Sierra Ravine. By Roger Starbuck.
105 **Minonee,** the Wood Witch; or, The Squatter's Secret. By Edwin Emerson.
106 **The Boy Cruisers;** or, Joe and Jap's Big Find. By Edward Willett.
107 **The Border Rovers;** or, Lost on the Overland Trail. By J. Milton Hoffman.
108 **Alaska,** the Wolf-Queen; or, The Girty Brothers' Double Crime. By Capt. Howard Lincoln.
109 **Christian Jim,** the White Man's Friend. By Edward S. Ellis.
110 **Plucky Joe,** the Boy Avenger; or, Dick Belmont's Last Ride. By J. Milton Hoffman.
111 **The Border Gunmaker;** or, The Hunted Maiden. By James L. Bowen.
112 **Left-Handed Pete,** the Double-Knife. By Joseph E. Badger, Jr.
113 **The River Rifles;** or, The Fate of the Flatboat. By Capt. J. F. C. Adams.
114 **Alone on the Plains.** By Edward Willett.
115 **Silver Horn,** and His Rifle Firedeath. By Roger Starbuck.
116 **Exploits of Hezekiah Smith,** the Backwoodsman. By Emerson Rodman.
117 **The Young Mustangers;** or, Dick Merry's Rangers. By C. Dunning Clark.
118 **Old Traps;** or, the Boy Rivals. By Barry Ringgold.
119 **Center Shot,** the White Crow; or, Roving Rifle's First Campaign. By T. C. Harbaugh.
120 **A Hot Trail;** or, Clark Cloverly Among the Tartars. By Charles Morris.
121 **Hunter Pard Ben;** or, The Wakash's Blind Lead. By Roger Starbuck.
122 **The Esquimaux' Queen;** or, The Mystery of the Lone Hut. By G. Waldo Browne.
123 **Tim,** the Boy Acrobat; or, Life in the Circus Ring. By Charles Morris.
124 **Queen Bessie,** the Border Girl. By Henry J. Thomas.
125 **Tom Tabor,** the Boy Fugitive; or, The Young Lynch-Gang "Wolves." By Barry Ringgold.
126 **Mink Coat,** the Death-Shot; or, The Spring of the Tiger. By Jos. E. Badger, Jr.
127 **The Deer Hunters.** By John J. Marshall.
128 **Wolf-Cap;** or, The Night-Hawks of the Fire-Lands. By Capt. Chas. Howard.
129 **Silverspur;** or, The Mountain Heroine. By Edward Willett.
130 **Keetsea,** Queen of the Plains. By Percy B. St. John.
131 **Wistah,** the Child Spy. By George Gleason.
132 **The Island Trapper;** or, The Young White-Buffalo Hunters. By Charles Howard.
133 **The Forest Specter;** or, The Young Hunter's Foe. By Edward Willett.
134 **Wild Nat,** the Trooper. By Wm. R. Eyster.
135 **The Silver Bugle;** or, The Indian Maiden of St. Croix. By Lieut. Col. Hazelton.
136 **The Prairie Trapper.** By C. Dunning Clark.
137 **The Antelope Boy.** By Geo. L. Aiken.
138 **Long Shot;** or, The Dwarf Guide. By Capt. Comstock.
139 **Colonel Crockett,** the Bear King. By Charles E. Lasalle.
140 **Old Pegs,** the Mountaineer; or, The Trapper Rivals. By Lewis W. Carson.
141 **The Giant Hunter;** or, The Mad Scourge of the Kickapoos. By Harry Hazard.
142 **Black Panther,** the Half-Blood. By Joseph E. Badger, Jr.
143 **Carson,** the Guide; or, Perils of the Frontier. By Lieut. J. H. Randolph.
144 **Kent,** the Ranger; or, The Fugitives of the Border. By Edward S. Ellis. Ready Jan. 15.
145 **Bill Robbins,** Hunter; or, The Man in Green. By Edward Willett. Ready Jan. 22.
146 **The Half-Breed Rival;** or, The Tangled Trail. By Jos. E. Badger, Jr. Ready Jan. 29.
147 **The Masked Avenger.** By Col. Prentiss Ingraham. Ready Feb. 5.
148 **Nat,** the Trapper and Indian Fighter. By Paul J. Prescott. Ready Feb. 12.

Beadle's Boy's Library is for sale by all Newsdealers, five cents per copy, or sent by mail on receipt of six cents each.

BEADLE AND ADAMS, Publishers,
98 William Street, New York.

Printed by Libri Plureos GmbH in Hamburg, Germany